experience and a passion for travel.

Rely on Thomas Cook as your travelling companion on your next trip and benefit from our unique heritage.

Thomas Cook **pocket** guides

BELFAST

Your travelling companion since 1873

Thomas Cook

Written and updated by Louise McGrath

Published by Thomas Cook Publishing
A division of Thomas Cook Tour Operations Limited
Company registration no. 3772199 England
The Thomas Cook Business Park, Unit 9, Coningsby Road,
Peterborough PE3 8SB, United Kingdom
Email: books@thomascook.com, Tel: + 44 (0) 1733 416477
www.thomascookpublishing.com

Produced by Cambridge Publishing Management Limited
Burr Elm Court, Main Street, Caldecote CB23 7NU
www.cambridgepm.co.uk

ISBN: 978-1-84848-347-7

osi Ordnance Survey Ireland

Series Editor: Karen Beaulah
Production/DTP: Steven Collins

Printed and bound in Spain by GraphyCems

Cover photography © David Robertson/Alamy

CONTENTS

SYMBOLS KEY

The following symbols are used throughout this book:

address telephone fax website address email opening times public transport connections important

The following symbols are used on the maps:

information office	point of interest
airport	city
hospital	large town
police station	small town
bus station	motorway
railway station	main road
cathedral	minor road
numbers denote featured cafés & restaurants	railway
	footpath

Hotels and restaurants are graded by approximate price as follows:

£ budget price **££** mid-range price **£££** expensive

Morning calm over the Lagan Weir

INTRODUCING
Belfast

Introduction

Belfast is buzzing. Not since the height of the Industrial Revolution, when it was given its city status by Queen Victoria, has it seen such a period of optimism. And in spite of the recent downturn, Belfast's economy has been cushioned by the crowds who flood north from the Republic of Ireland looking for a bargain. For the past decade the city has been shaking off its violent image and projecting itself as a vibrant place with plenty to offer the visitor, from art, history and green spaces to fine dining, café culture and trendy bars. Even the notorious Falls and Shankill roads are seeing a piece of the new action, with sightseeing buses and 'ex-prisoner' tours taking visitors to the political murals of West Belfast.

Belfast is the largest city in Northern Ireland, but with a relatively small population the urban area can easily be explored on foot. It's also not difficult to get out of the city for a day or two if you want to head north along the stunning Antrim Coast to Giant's Causeway or south to County Down and the Mourne Mountains.

From the landmark City Hall in Donegall Square you can shop your way along Royal Avenue, over to the Cathedral Quarter and along High Street to Custom House Square. You can enjoy riverside walks along the Lagan, picnics in the Botanic Gardens and mini hikes to McArt's Fort in Cave Hill Country Park. There's interactive fun at the Odyssey complex, classical concerts at the Waterfront Hall and live bands at the Limelight. Tuck into an Ulster fry for breakfast, snack on seafood chowder and wheaten bread for lunch and sample

some modern Irish cuisine for dinner, then bar hop down the Golden Mile to Botanic Avenue for some of that notorious Irish *craic*.

These days there's little to keep you away from Belfast. Its new-found optimism has meant regeneration and an increase in the number of budget airlines flying to the two nearby airports.

Waterfront Hall from the River Lagan

When to go

Although sunstroke won't be a major worry, summer days can be lovely, and the warmth of the welcome from the local people will soothe even the wettest winter chill. Belfast's manifold charms are not weather-dependent. Swing by any time: you'll love it.

SEASONS & CLIMATE

Located in Belfast Lough, which leads out to the Irish Sea, Belfast has a temperate maritime climate, with four distinct seasons. The general vibe tends towards the moist, with an annual rainfall of 85 cm (33½ in). Summer temperatures average around 17.5°C (63.5°F); winter temperatures around 6°C (43°F).

Crowds flock to open-air concerts at City Hall

ANNUAL EVENTS

January

Out to Lunch Brought to you by the organisers of May's Cathedral Quarter Arts Festival (see below), this is a city-wide, month-long arts festival, of comedy, theatre, music and literary talks, that turns up many a gem. ⓦ www.cqaf.com

March

St Patrick's Day (17 Mar) Belfast's city-centre celebrations for Ireland's patron saint started in 1998. These days the carnival parade moves swiftly through the city centre to Custom House Square, where renowned musicians perform on stage.

May

Cathedral Quarter Arts Festival Fringe theatre and performing arts groups, as well as music, comedy, film, circus acts and visual arts events, take over the city's pubs and arts venues for the month. ⓦ www.cqaf.com

The Balmoral Show (Usually mid-month) Ireland's largest agricultural show, featuring a children's farm, dog agility competitions, falconry displays, livestock, Pony Club games, sheep shearing, showjumping and gun dog displays. ⓐ Balmoral Showgrounds ⓦ www.balmoralshow.co.uk

June

Beat Summer Carnival (Late June) A cross-community event in Custom House Square, with a carnival parade, floats, bands, dancers and cultural groups from diverse sections of the community. ⓣ 028 9046 0865 ⓦ www.belfastcarnival.com

July

Orangefest On 12 July the Orange Order celebrates the victory of William of Orange over James I in 1690 with 'demonstrations'. The Belfast demonstrations are the largest in Northern Ireland and see Orange Order flute bands parading through the city centre and south to Edenderry Field for speeches. To appeal to a wider audience, the event has been rebranded as 'Orangefest'. This celebration of Ulster culture has become increasingly family-friendly, with face-painting, bouncy castles and stilt walkers.

Belfast International Rose Trials and Rose Week at Sir Thomas and Lady Dixon Park (Late July) This attracts 50,000 visitors for the serious rose competition as well as fun activities for children, from face-painting to treasure hunts.
Ⓦ www.belfastcity.gov.uk/parksandopenspaces/roseweek.asp

Belfast Pride Mainly – but not exclusively – gay-themed jamboree that sees a week of artistic and cultural events culminating in a colourful parade through the city centre. Ⓦ www.belfastpride.com

August

West Belfast Festival (Féile an Phobail) The largest community-led festival in Europe, with internationally renowned musicians, exhibitions, debates, drama events, an international food fair and a parade. Ⓦ www.feilebelfast.com

September

Open House Festival (Late Sept) The Cathedral Quarter celebrates the Open House Festival: traditional arts with a focus on music events from Irish traditional to bluegrass, Cajun and country.
Ⓦ www.openhousefestival.com

October

Belfast Festival at Queen's Ireland's largest arts festival comes to Queen's each year, with an impressive programme of events featuring renowned and up-and-coming performers and artists, cutting-edge performances and special projects in theatre, dance, music, visual art, film and spoken word throughout the city. ⓦ www.belfastfestival.com

November

Belfast Book Fair Book lovers flock here for the country's biggest and longest-running book fair, with dozens of dealers doing a good trade in second-hand, rare and antiquarian publications. ⓣ 028 9038 1111 ⓦ www.belfastbookfair.com

CineMagic World Screen Festival for Young People Month-long, city-wide screen fest for children. ⓦ www.cinemagic.org.uk

PUBLIC HOLIDAYS

New Year's Day 1 Jan

St Patrick's Day 17 Mar

Good Friday 22 Apr 2011; 6 Apr 2012; 29 Mar 2013

Easter Monday 25 Apr 2011; 9 Apr 2012; 1 Apr 2013

May Bank Holiday first Mon in May

Spring Bank Holiday last Mon in May

Battle of the Boyne 12 July

August Bank Holiday last Mon in Aug

Christmas Day 25 Dec

Boxing Day 26 Dec

Rebirth of Belfast

The new optimism felt in Belfast since the 1998 Good Friday Agreement and devolution in 2007 has resonated throughout the city, attracting investment into run-down areas. The first 'new builds' included the BT Tower, Hilton Hotel and apartments on Laganside, plus the landmark Odyssey Complex and Science Park, which have made inroads into the Titanic Quarter. In 2008 the multi-million-pound Victoria Square shopping centre opened in the heart of Belfast. The centre is an architectural masterpiece that blends Belfast's Victorian architecture with 21st-century style, and adds to its attractiveness as a destination for city breaks.

The redevelopment of the former Gasworks 'brown site' into a landscaped showpiece with offices, the Radisson Hotel, housing and cafés has been hailed as a major success. Custom House Square has also had a makeover, giving it new life and opening it up to live events and festivals. The Grand Opera House has been extended and improved, and the former Ulster Bank in the Cathedral Quarter has been transformed into the elegant Merchant Hotel.

The residential Obel Tower on Laganside is the city's latest showpiece – at 85 m (279 ft) high, it is Ireland's tallest skyscraper – and new nightlife and entertainment venues are to follow in the area.

The Ulster Museum rejuvenation project has brought a fresh entrance and arrival space, improved history and natural science galleries and new rooftop gallery, café and restaurant. As the Old Museum Arts Centre awaits its move to a purpose-built site in the Cathedral Quarter in 2011, the Lyric Theatre has been tirelessly raising money to complete its new home in Stranmillis.

Meanwhile, City Hall's prized Victorian interior has undergone some vital maintenance.

The regeneration and construction that has already taken place is just the beginning. Over the next two decades the Titanic Quarter is to be transformed into a new maritime quarter, adding cafés and bars, retail space, apartments, hotel and office buildings, as well as a new quay at Abercorn Basin, community facilities, and public art and event spaces.

The city centre was a virtual no-go area at night before the Good Friday Agreement. While the political future is still being defined, construction and regeneration of the city has made its residents feel a sense of renewal. Tourists generally feel happier to visit Belfast and it has become one of the hottest city-break destinations in the United Kingdom.

Regeneration continues to transform the city centre

History

Belfast's name derives from the Gaelic *Béal Feirste*, meaning 'sandy ford at the mouth of the River Farset'. The location of the Farset, now contained within a pipe under High Street, is the oldest part of the city. Baron Arthur Chichester built a castle here in 1611, although it was destroyed in a fire in 1708.

Chichester encouraged the plantation of Ulster by English and Scottish Protestant Planters, but during the Irish Uprising of 1641, thousands of these Planters were massacred, and many fled back to England. James II became king of Ireland in 1685, but the arrival of William of Orange saw support by Ulster, where there was a Protestant majority. James was defeated in 1690 and penal laws were brought in, curbing the rights of Catholics.

By the early 18th century Belfast was a large settlement with the arrival of French Huguenots stimulating the growth of its linen industry. One of their descendants, the philanthropist and radical Henry Joy McCracken, formed the United Irishmen with Theobold Wolfe Tone. Their aim was to end oppressive English rule, but following their 1798 rebellion at the Battle of Antrim, McCracken was captured and hanged.

During the 19th century the Industrial Revolution led to growth in shipbuilding, ropeworks, tobacco factories and linen mills and Belfast receiving city status by royal decree. New employment opportunities, together with the devastating effects of the potato famine in rural areas, meant thousands of people flooded there. Unrest continued into the new century, and following the Irish War of Independence, most of Ulster saw partition from the south and the creation of Northern Ireland with Belfast as its capital.

The city continued to grow, becoming the world's most important shipbuilding location. However, Belfast was severely bombed during World War II, and the post-war period saw jobs disappearing as air travel began to supersede sea travel.

Old religious prejudices led to civil rights marches by Catholics and riots by loyalist gangs, culminating in the British Army's deployment to keep the peace in 1969. Direct rule by the British government replaced the Northern Ireland government and the period known as the Troubles continued for almost 30 years, with violence by the IRA, the loyalist UVF and other paramilitary groups. After peace talks with republican party Sinn Féin, and an IRA ceasefire, the Good Friday Agreement was put into place in 1998, leading to the creation of the Northern Ireland Assembly. This was suspended by the British Government in 2002, but after years of negotiations devolution of power was achieved in 2007. Under the power-sharing agreement, Peter Robinson has been first minister since 2008, despite both scandal and having lost his seat as an MP in Westminster.

Stormont parliament buildings, home to the Northern Ireland Assembly

Lifestyle

In the past decade the city centre has undergone a physical transformation and the lifestyle of many of Belfast's residents has also improved. The city centre is now open and vibrant with a booming café culture, new bars, restaurants, shops and cultural venues. Even the Falls and Shankill roads have become attractions as tourists take guided tours to see the political murals, something that would have seemed unlikely little more than a decade ago. Despite this, the political future remains uncertain, and with the Troubles still in the memories of most of the population, old rivalries and fears persist.

Many children still go to Catholic or Protestant schools and therefore identity is defined by community, with sports, music, language and even one's football team dictated by education and religion. Growing numbers of integrated schools and cross-community projects are working tirelessly to promote mutual understanding and transcend these rivalries.

In the Cathedral Quarter, city centre and South Belfast you really have a feel of this transformation, and there is an excitement about the changes and the benefits of a newly affluent society. Students from both communities meet at college and begin to understand each other, while equal opportunities at work have also led to further integration and tolerance.

While there is still a long way to go and some issues may never be resolved, Belfast is buzzing. People enjoy the same lifestyle as those in the rest of the UK, working and playing hard, particularly now they can freely go out after work in the city centre to enjoy the new generation of restaurants, fringe theatre and bars, plus late-night shopping on a Thursday and drinking along the Golden Mile on a Friday. The cost of living is more or less the same as the rest of the UK, but you might find that bars, restaurants and hotels are cheaper than in London.

Most people are happy to show visitors around their city, but just be careful about being over-curious about politics and religion, as these are sensitive subjects, and avoid wearing football shirts that might attract negative attention. Let the locals show you the murals or talk about their personal views and orientations if they like; otherwise, take in the history at the museums and on the tour bus, and enjoy a large helping of the *craic* at the pub.

Belfast has a thriving pub culture

Culture

The official language of the Republic of Ireland, the Irish language or Gaelic (*Gaeilge*), is recognised as their native language by a large percentage of the nationalist community. It's taught in Catholic schools as well as at the Gaelic language centre in the Falls Road, Cultúrlann McAdam (see page 85). The church has traditionally been the hub of the community for Catholic residents and a unifying force through the Troubles. Today, Mass attendance at Catholic churches has fallen to an all-time low in West Belfast, but there the church is still a regular meeting point for dance and music groups, where children (and adults) can learn traditional Irish dancing and how to play instruments heard in traditional Irish music, including the fiddle, mandolin, *bodhrán* and tin whistle. Gaelic football and hurling clubs are also affiliated with the church (see page 33). You often know when you're in a Catholic or nationalist neighbourhood as many of the shop signs will be in Celtic script or even in Irish. You can see dancing on St Patrick's Day and in arts centres. The best place to hear traditional music is in pubs. Celtic art is exhibited in arts centres and the Gaelic language centre and you can buy it from the Wicker Man on High Street.

Other cultural forms have developed in spite of the turbulent past, particularly with the investment in arts centres and venues such as the Waterfront Hall (see page 67). Home to the Ulster Orchestra, it also stages classical music and operatic performances. In 2010 the Arts Council announced the creation of Opera Company NI, a new musical venture that aims to raise the profile of the genre in the province over the next few years.

The 2,250-seater auditorium at Waterfront Hall

THE HAMELY TONGUE

As part of the Good Friday Agreement, it was agreed that 'respect and understanding and tolerance' would be given to the Ulster-Scots language. Also known as Ullans, Ulster-Scots is a variant of Scots that developed among the descendants of the Planters from Scotland since the 16th century and is spoken by an estimated 100,000 people in Northern Ireland. It was actually recognised as a language back in 1992. The Ulster Scots Agency promotes the study, development and use of the language and culture by publishing contemporary writing and providing teaching resources for schools. Speaking of the language has also meant a rise in other cultural forms associated with the Ulster Scots peoples, including music and literature. Many Ulster Scots events take place in Orange Halls. See the **Ulster Scots Agency** website (Ⓦ www.ulsterscotsagency.com) for a list of upcoming events.

The Albert Clock and Custom House from the Lagan

MAKING THE MOST OF
Belfast

Shopping

Belfast has plenty of opportunities for shopping and spending. All the usual high-street stores can be found along Donegall Place, Royal Avenue and the streets leading off it, especially Donegall Square North, Wellington Place, Upper Queen Street and Howard Street to the west, and Rosemary Street, Bridge Street, Castle Place, Cornmarket, Arthur Street, William Street and Ann Street to the east. **Marks and Spencer** (t 028 9023 5235) can be found at the bottom of Donegall Place and **Dunnes Stores** (t 028 9041 7880) along Cornmarket. For high-quality traditional Irish gifts and crafts, the **Wicker Man** (t 028 9024 3550) on High Street is unsurpassed.

The **Spires Mall** on Wellington Street has a dozen or so shops, as does **Donegall Arcade** (a Castle Place), which has been refurbished and extended and now includes a huge TK Maxx store at its former back entrance, on Rosemary Street.

The **Victoria Square shopping centre** (w www.victoriasquare.com) opened in 2008 and is a showpiece with its glass dome and viewing platform, several new restaurants and a range of high-street and designer stores. **CastleCourt** (a Royal Avenue) remains a popular shopping centre, with emphasis on high-street fashion and a choice of fast-food eateries. For designer boutiques and upmarket home-ware stores, head to Lisburn Road, and to Boucher Road for several large furniture, DIY and fashion outlets.

Out of town, you'll find Marks and Spencer's third-largest store at **Sprucefield** (w www.sprucefieldcentre.co.uk), and factory outlets **Junction One** (a Off junction 1 of the M1 motorway) and **The Outlet** (ⓐ Banbridge on the A1), which opened in 2007. Both places offer all sorts of bargains, from clothes to home wares and toys.

The distinctive dome of the Victoria Square shopping centre

Eating & drinking

There's little chance of avoiding an Ulster fry when you visit Belfast, although since it features mostly sausages, bacon and black or white pudding (along with soda bread, potato farls, fried eggs and sometimes mushrooms), vegetarians might be a bit put off. These days there are a few more vegetarian options, including plenty of cereals and some smoothie bars, but you'll need to shop around. Once you're set up with a good breakfast you'll not be wanting for anything for quite some time, and most locals usually grab a sandwich or light lunch. There are plenty of coffee shops and snack bars opening where you can have a doorstep sandwich, soup and wheaten bread or two-course lunch specials. Lunch is generally called 'dinner' and after work you go home for your 'tea', although plenty of people stay out in the city centre after work and there are numerous dining options.

In traditional restaurants you'll find dishes such as Irish stew (once made from mutton but today from lamb, carrots and onions), sausage and champ (creamy mashed potato with scallions – spring onions), and boiled bacon (ham) and cabbage. There's usually plenty of meat on the menu, including succulent plates of Irish beef, pork and lamb. You also can't miss the fresh

PRICE CATEGORIES
Price ratings in this book are based on the average price of a two-course meal for one without drinks.
£ up to £15 **££** £15–25 **£££** over £25

fish and seafood with warm bowls of seafood chowder and wheaten bread, fresh prawns, herrings, mackerel, lobster, oysters and mussels from the sea, and freshwater fish such as salmon and trout. As you head up the Antrim Coast or south towards Strangford Lough and the Mournes, you'll find a greater selection of fish on the menu. Chinese and Italian restaurants have been popular in Belfast for decades, but the city's new positive image is attracting other international restaurants serving Japanese, Spanish and Indian cuisine.

Instead of spending a fortune in restaurants you could opt for a picnic, if the weather is good. Pick up some bread, cheese and ham from St George's Market (see page 68) and head to the City Hall gardens or out to Ormean Park or the Botanic Gardens.

Bread plays an important part in the Belfast diet and there are many varieties to choose from: potato bread (made from mashed potato), soda farls (raised with bicarbonate of soda rather than yeast), barm brack (fruit soda, a traditional bread to eat toasted on Halloween), boxty (made from potato, flour, egg and bicarb and said to have emerged during the potato famine), plain loaf (white sliced bread) and the good old crusty Belfast bap (bread roll). The high level of milk production in Northern Ireland means plenty of dairy products too, from creamy fresh butter to strong hard cheese. Look out for locally produced goat's milk and cheese – you'll be able to pick some up at St George's Market.

All that bread will need to be washed down with a few drinks. Tea is very popular here, with buttered wheaten or toasted barm brack, and you'll want to try the famous Irish coffee, but in the end there's no excuse needed to head out for a few pints.

Apartment: one of the most fashionable eateries in town

The most famous Irish beverage is Guinness®, which is drunk plentifully in Belfast, but cider is also popular. Armagh is known as the orchard county and you might pick up some home-made cider in the organic market, but in the pubs it will come from the Republic of Ireland. Known as Bulmer's (not to be confused with the English Bulmer's) in the South, in Northern Ireland and the rest of the UK it is marketed as Magners. There has been a huge surge in sales in the past few years and you'll see plenty of large bottles (or draught) sold. Drink it in a pint glass with plenty of ice – they say it helps rehydrate you! If that's not enough, finish with a few drams of Bushmills Irish Whiskey as a nightcap.

A RESTAURANT REVOLUTION

The development of the city centre has led to the evolution of a modern Irish cuisine, spearheaded by celebrity chefs such as Paul Rankin and Michael Deane. What makes the food modern is the variation on traditional dishes or an international twist with Asian, Mediterranean, Latin American or other influences in the ingredients. Expect pale smoked haddock risotto and Indian-spiced loin of lamb from Rankin, and glazed breast of Gressingham duck with pak choi, gingerbread, potato fondant and spiced port from Deane.

Entertainment & nightlife

Socialising plays a big part in Belfast life, from dinner and drinks to a full-on pub crawl, theatre and classical orchestras to traditional Irish music and fringe performing arts groups. There are no rules on where and when you should go out, except the licensing laws, although these too have relaxed in some areas, with some pubs staying open until midnight at the weekends and clubs until 02.00 or 03.00. Evening films usually start between 18.00 and 21.00, concerts and shows around 20.00 and gigs around 21.00.

At the Belfast Welcome Centre (see page 136) you can pick up a copy of *Whatabout*, which has listings for music and entertainment, pubs and clubs, theatre, opera and comedy, as well as family entertainment, shopping, eating and attractions. Also look out for a copy of *FATE*, which gives a round-up of the coolest bars, clubs, fashion and music.

For gentle, upmarket bars, stay in the Cathedral Quarter, city centre and South Belfast, where hotel bars offer snacks and evening drinks, sometimes with music. There is equally a crop of bars for the more mature and discerning crowd, including the likes of Café Vaudeville on Arthur St (see page 72). If you want something more down to earth, head to the Golden Mile, where pubs from Robinson's (see page 73) and the Crown Liquor Saloon (see page 72) down to Shaftesbury Square offer lively nights. Students and younger crowds also hang out in the Botanic Avenue and Ormeau Road areas, where you'll find plenty of busy bars and pubs. The trendier crowd hang out in bars along the Lisburn Road. For clubbing, you're talking about much the same

You're never far from a good pint in Belfast

Fibber Magee's hosts regular gigs (see page 73)

areas, along Ormeau Avenue, Botanic Avenue, Shaftesbury Square and Cathedral Quarter around Donegall Street. For a gay bar, try Mynt on Dunbar Street (see page 73) in the Cathedral Quarter.

There's absolutely no shortage of music in Belfast, with something for everyone from traditional folk through to thrash metal, nu rave and indie. Just pick up the free listings magazines (see page 28) and see what inflates your Uilleann pipes. You can hear classical music and opera at the Waterfront Hall (see page 67), along with big-name concerts. The Ulster Orchestra and jazz groups play at the Ulster Hall in Bedford Street (see page 67). The best places to catch the very latest bands are The Limelight and Spring & Airbrake (see page 73). You can hear live traditional music in Fibber Magee's (see page 73), The John Hewitt (see page 72) and Cultúrlann McAdam (see page 85), among others. During the warmer months there are open-air concerts outside the City Hall (see pages 63–4), in Custom House Square and in the Botanic Gardens.

The only full-time producing theatre in Northern Ireland was demolished, but work is well under way on a new venue. Fringe centres such as Catalyst Arts (see page 66), Crescent Arts Centre (see page 97) and Old Museum Arts Centre (see page 67) also exhibit new artists and shows.

The Queen's Film Theatre (see page 98) shows a range of films in their original language with subtitles – screenings usually start between 18.00 and 21.00.

Your hotel should have a free booklet with the latest listings.

Sport & relaxation

SPECTATOR SPORTS

Football

The Irish League is the main NI league but it doesn't carry the same prestige as the leagues in England, Scotland and the rest of Europe. One of Belfast's main teams is Linfield FC, based at **Windsor Park** (ⓐ Windsor Park, Donegall Avenue), which is also the venue for the Northern Ireland team's international matches.

Irish League ⓦ http://irishpremierleague.com

Irish Football Association ⓦ www.irishfa.com

Catch great rugby at Ravenhill Stadium

Gaelic football

Gaelic football, a cross between football, rugby and war, is hugely popular among the Catholic community, with teams affiliated to church parishes. County Antrim trains and holds its home games at **Casement Park** (t 028 9060 5868) on Falls Road. It's not a game for the faint-hearted but can be very entertaining to watch.

Horse racing

Northern Ireland's premier racecourse is **Down Royal Racecourse** (a 24 Ballyduggan Road, Downpatrick w www.downroyal.com) at Downpatrick. There are regular fixtures throughout the year and tickets are available online.

Hurling

As with Gaelic football, Belfast's hurling teams are affiliated to the local parishes. Once again, Casement Park is the venue for the County Antrim team's home games.

Ice hockey

The **Belfast Giants** (w www.belfastgiants.co.uk) are the major team in the city and their base is at the **Odyssey Arena** (a Odyssey Arena, Queen's Quay t 028 9703 9074 w www.odysseyarena.com), where the home Elite League games are played against other UK teams.

Rugby

Ravenhill Stadium (a Ravenhill Stadium, Ravenhill) is home to **Ulster Rugby** (w www.ulsterrugby.ie), which has stayed in the Irish Rugby Football Union since partition in 1921, meaning six of the nine counties of the Ulster branch are in Northern Ireland

and three are in the Republic of Ireland. So you can expect to see games against Leinster, Munster and Connacht, as well as teams from Scotland, England and Wales.

PARTICIPATION SPORTS

Belfast has numerous sports centres run by the city council, as well as private gyms and health clubs, including **Fitness First** (ⓦ www.fitnessfirst.co.uk), **LA Fitness** (ⓦ www.lafitness.co.uk) and **LivingWell Health Club** (ⓦ www.livingwell.com).

Golf

Northern Ireland is a popular destination for golf and there are several courses within easy reach of Belfast, including **Hilton Templepatrick Golf Club** (ⓦ www.hilton.co.uk/templepatrick), **Royal Belfast Golf Club** in Holywood (ⓦ www.royalbelfast.com) and **Royal County Down** in Newcastle (ⓦ www.royalcountydown.org).

Outdoor & adventure sports

Close to Belfast you can go walking in **Colin Glen Forest Park** (ⓦ www.colinglentrust.org), along the Lagan Towpath to Lisburn (see pages 89–92) or in Cave Hill Country Park (see page 80). For longer treks, head to the Glens of Antrim (see page 121) or the Mourne Mountains (see page 110). In the Mournes you can also go climbing and orienteering, with courses at **Tollymore Mountain Centre** (ⓦ www.tollymore.com). **One Great Adventure** (ⓦ www.onegreatadventure.com) runs adventure days plus courses and practice days in canoeing, climbing, bouldering, camp craft, mountain biking and much more.

Accommodation

In general, accommodation in Belfast costs around the same as in other parts of the UK, but there's a variety of places to stay, and with the city's booming development, new hotels are opening fairly regularly. It's best to book somewhere in advance. The tourist office website (ⓦ www.gotobelfast.com) has a 'special offers' section, as well as full listings of other accommodation according to classification. Also try the **Northern Ireland Tourist Board** (ⓦ www.visitnorthernireland.com) and **Tourism Ireland** (ⓦ www.discoverireland.com). There are several websites offering online bookings, often with discounts; some of the best include ⓦ www.goireland.com, www.expedia.co.uk, www.hotels.co.uk, www.opodo.co.uk and www.hini.org.uk

If you find yourself in Belfast without anywhere to stay, the staff in the Belfast Welcome Centre in Donegall Place (see page 136) are very helpful. Alternatively, try some of the suggestions below according to your taste and budget.

The best places to stay are in the city centre along the streets around Donegall Square, along Great Victoria Street to Shaftesbury Square, Botanic, Stranmillis and Malone in South Belfast. There are some large hotels such as the Hilton, by the Waterfront Hall,

PRICE CATEGORIES

Gradings used in this book are based on the average price for a double room per night, including breakfast.

£ up to £60 **££** £60–100 **£££** over £100

and the Radisson in the old gasworks south of St George's Market. Recently opened in the Cathedral Quarter is a new Premier Inn, and nearby the luxury Merchant Hotel is being extended. You can find places to stay in other parts of Belfast, including along the Antrim Road in North Belfast, Dunmurry in West Belfast and Stormont in East Belfast, but for easy access to attractions it's easier and safer to stay more centrally. For out-of-town options, see the relevant chapters of this book or the websites on page 35.

HOTELS

Premier Inn £–££ One of the best of the budget hotels, this branch is located in the up-and-coming Cathedral Quarter, with most city-centre attractions, as well as bars and restaurants, within walking distance. ⓐ 2–6 Waring Street ⓣ 0871 527 8070 ⓦ www.premierinn.com ⓝ Bus: Laganside Buscentre

Benedict's ££ Located at the top end of Belfast's Golden Mile, this trendy hotel has a gothic-themed bar, live DJs and music, and slick guest rooms with modern décor. ⓐ 7–21 Bradbury Place, Shaftesbury Square ⓣ 028 9059 1999 ⓦ www.benedictshotel.co.uk ⓝ Bus: 8A, 7B

Days Hotel ££ Northern Ireland's largest hotel, with spacious and comfortable rooms. Located just off the Golden Mile. ⓐ 40 Hope Street ⓣ 028 9024 2494 ⓦ www.dayshotelbelfast.co.uk ⓝ Bus: Europa Buscentre; Train: Great Victoria Street

Holiday Inn Belfast ££ Located in the heart of Belfast's Golden Mile with contemporary rooms, restaurant and bar. ⓐ 22 Ormeau

Avenue ⓣ 0870 400 9005 ⓕ 028 9062 6546 ⓦ www.ichotelsgroup.com Train: Great Victoria Street

Madison's ££ Small stylish hotel with bar, restaurant and club, this is a favourite with rock bands and is located in the heart of lively Botanic. ⓐ 59–63 Botanic Avenue ⓣ 028 9050 9800 ⓦ www.madisonshotel.com Bus: 7A-B, 8A-B

Stormont Hotel ££ Overlooks the Northern Ireland government grounds in the east of the city and has two restaurants. ⓐ Upper Newtownards Road ⓣ 028 9027 1066 ⓦ www.hastingshotels.com Bus: 20A

The Crescent Townhouse Hotel £££ Intimate and stylish hotel located in the heart of the cool Botanic area, with canopy beds and Victorian-style roll-top baths, plus a brasserie and bar. ⓐ 13 Lower Crescent ⓣ 028 9032 3349 ⓦ www.crescenttownhouse.com Bus: 7

Europa Hotel £££ Renowned as 'the most bombed hotel in Europe', but don't worry – that dates back to the Troubles. It remains one of the best hotels in the city, located next to the Grand Opera House and opposite the Crown Liquor Saloon. ⓐ Great Victoria Street ⓣ 028 9027 1066 ⓕ 028 9032 7800 ⓦ www.hastingshotels.com Bus: Europa Buscentre

Hilton Belfast £££ Located next to the Waterfront Hall, this 5-star hotel has impressive facilities, including restaurants, bars, riverside views and a health club. ⓐ 4 Lanyon Place

t 028 9027 7000 w www.hilton.co.uk/belfast
e reservations.belfast@hilton.com Bus: Laganside Buscentre

Malmaison £££ You'll find stylish and slinky guest rooms here or large suites named after the cranes that helped build the *Titanic*. The hotel also has a brasserie, bar and gym. a 34–38 Victoria Street t 0845 365 4247 w www.malmaison-belfast.com e belfast@malmaison.com Bus: Donegall Square/Royal Avenue

The Merchant Hotel: luxury in the heart of the city

Merchant Hotel £££ This swanky hotel was once the headquarters of the Ulster Bank; the 19th-century building has been transformed to include luxury accommodation. You can also pop in for traditional afternoon tea, dinner and drinks. ⓐ 35–39 Waring Street ⓣ 028 9023 4888 ⓦ www.themerchanthotel.com Bus: Laganside Buscentre

Radisson Blu Hotel £££ Modern, comfortable hotel with a restaurant, bar and large car park. ⓐ The Gasworks, Cromac Place ⓣ 028 9043 4065 ⓦ www.radisson.com Bus: 77, 30

Ten Square £££ Chic, central boutique hotel with Asian-style guest rooms, low-level beds and rich, cream carpets. ⓐ 10 Donegall Square South (City Centre) ⓣ 028 9024 1001 ⓦ www.tensquare.co.uk ⓔ reservations@tensquare.co.uk Bus: Donegall Square

YOUTH HOSTELS

Arnies Backpackers £ Located near Queen's University in the south of the city, you'll be near all the nightlife and won't have to pay a packet. ⓐ 63 Fitzwilliam Street ⓣ 028 9024 2867 ⓦ www.arniesbackpackers.co.uk Bus: 8A-B

Belfast International Youth Hostel £ Located right on Belfast's Golden Mile, this hostel is well located for sightseeing and going out. ⓐ 22–32 Donegall Road ⓣ 028 9031 5435 ⓦ www.hini.org.uk Bus: 8A, 7B

THE BEST OF BELFAST

There's a lot to see and do in Belfast, but if you've only got a few hours or days to spare, try some of the following must-sees.

TOP 10 ATTRACTIONS

- **Belfast Citysightseeing bus tour** A good introduction to Belfast, covering the city centre and nearby attractions (see page 58).
- **City Hall** The city centre's most prominent landmark: step inside to see the elaborate interior or picnic in the gardens (see pages 63–4).
- **Ulster Museum** A treasure trove of history, science and art, giving a thorough insight into Northern Ireland's past and present (see page 98).
- **Crown Liquor Saloon** One of the oldest and most elaborate bars in the city – sit in a 'snug' with a pint of Guinness® (see page 64).

- **Shopping spree** Pick up killer bargains at St George's Market (see page 68) and designer labels from the Victoria Square shopping centre (see page 22).
- **Concert at Waterfront Hall** Belfast's primary concert hall hosts the Ulster Orchestra plus opera and comedy (see page 67).
- **West Belfast Murals** Book a guided tour or take in the political murals at your own pace (see pages 84–5).
- **Belfast Walking Tour** Visit the key places associated with RMS *Titanic*, including the SS *Nomadic* and drawing offices (see page 88).
- **W5 at Odyssey** An interactive discovery centre with scientific experiments, creative challenges and feats of physical strength (see page 92).
- **Hit the town** Bar hop down the Golden Mile – start in the city centre and head towards Shaftesbury Square and the Botanic area (see pages 72–3).

The opulent Crown Liquor Saloon

Suggested itineraries

HALF-DAY: BELFAST IN A HURRY

If you've only a few hours free, hop on a Belfast Citysightseeing bus tour (see page 58). In 90 minutes you'll get a flavour of the city centre, Cathedral Quarter (see page 63), Titanic Quarter (see pages 94–6), West Belfast Murals (see pages 84–5), University District (see page 88) and Golden Mile/nightlife (see page 28). If you've time left, jump off at the Europa Hotel (see page 37) and cross the road to the Crown Liquor Saloon (see page 64) for a pint.

1 DAY: TIME TO SEE A LITTLE MORE

If you've got a whole day, load up on a carb-tastic Ulster fry then take the bus tour in the morning, stop for lunch in the Crown Liquor Saloon (see page 64) and then explore the city centre on foot. Enjoy a free tour around City Hall (see pages 63–4) and take a peek at the books in the Linen Hall Library (see page 66). If you've time, have a little wander up Royal Avenue to buy some souvenirs in the Belfast Welcome Centre (see page 136).

2–3 DAYS: TIME TO SEE MUCH MORE

Lucky you: this means you've got time to explore beyond the city centre. Depending on your interests, you can pursue one of the above suggestions in depth. An alternative idea is to go on a Belfast Walking Tour (see page 88), which tells the story of the ill-fated *Titanic*'s tragically short life. If the weather is good, why not spend the day out of town at the Ulster Folk & Transport Museum (see page 112)? There should also be time for an

afternoon's intensive shopping along Royal Avenue and at the Victoria Square shopping centre (see page 22) and a night out at Café Vaudeville (see page 72) for jazz and cocktails; alternatively, whooping it up at Fibber Magee's (see page 73) will give you a blast of some traditional Irish music; Botanic Avenue is the place to go for a more studenty vibe.

LONGER: ENJOYING BELFAST TO THE FULL

If you've more than a couple of days on your hands, expose yourself to the glory of the countryside and drive or book an organised tour outside the city. Some of the best days out include a motorised pootle along the stunning Antrim Coast to Giant's Causeway (see page 119) and Bushmills Distillery (see page 117). Another sublimely seductive notion would be a day in Downpatrick visiting the Cathedral (see pages 105 & 108), or Down County Museum (see page 108), or going for a bracing walk in the Mourne Mountains (see page 110) and a fish supper in Newcastle (see page 111).

Bus tours take in all the sights

Something for nothing

You don't have to spend a fortune getting to know Belfast as there are plenty of free or fairly cheap activities to keep you occupied. Your first stop should be the Belfast Welcome Centre (see page 136), where information, advice, maps and brochures are all free.

Start by exploring the city centre on foot. Tours of City Hall (see pages 63–4) and browsing the superb collection of books at the Linen Hall Library (see page 66) don't cost a penny. Take in top attractions such as the Albert Memorial Clock, Custom House Square, Grand Opera House and Crown Liquor Saloon (see pages 58–67). Then head south along Victoria Street to see the impressive Queen's University (see pages 93–4) and on to the Ulster Museum (see page 98).

If you're good on your feet, head up the Falls Road and spend some time looking at the numerous political murals that adorn the houses there. These beautifully executed – but, not surprisingly, rather visceral – expressions of socio-political feeling are a reminder of the sectarian divisions that came so close to destroying the city.

Next, pop into Cultúrlann McAdam, the Irish language and culture centre, where you can stop for a café lunch, hear locals speaking Gaelic and have a browse in the bookshop (see page 85). Don't get carried away by the warmth of the welcome and the heady magnetism of the culture: this is not the place to debut your tribute to *Riverdance* in the hope of securing investment.

On a good day, walk or cycle along the Lagan Towpath, which runs 16 km (10 miles) from Stranmillis in South Belfast to Lisburn in

County Down (see pages 89–92). The route runs along the riverbank through beautiful scenery, urban parkland and nature trails. If that's too far, then head for one of the city parks, including the Botanic Gardens for its impressive plant collections and relaxing lawns (see page 89), Cave Hill Country Park for Belfast Castle and panoramic city views (see page 80), the Japanese Garden at Sir Thomas and Lady Dixon Park, or Ormeau Park for woodland and wildlife (see page 93).

The Linen Hall Library: fascinating and free

When it rains

The likelihood of it raining when you're in Belfast is quite high, so you should really just take a raincoat and an umbrella and not let a few drops of rain stop you from enjoying the sights outdoors. The open-top buses are swapped for ones with roofs on rainy days, so you can still take a tour around the city. The same goes for Black Taxi Tours, but if you really want to get out of the rain, there's no shortage of options.

Take a tour round City Hall (see pages 63–4), which will last about an hour, and includes the grand staircase, oak council chamber, the ornate dome and other features of this classical Renaissance building. You can easily spend several hours in the Ulster Museum (see page 98), which has something for everyone, including art, archaeology, local history and natural science, plus special exhibitions.

The Odyssey (see pages 92–3) is a fantastic all-day option (especially good if you have children with you), and you can park your car there if you have one. Spend the morning getting hands-on in W5, an interactive centre of discovery, then have lunch in the Odyssey Pavilion before seeing a film at the IMAX cinema in the afternoon. You might even be able to catch a game by the Belfast Giants ice hockey team (see page 33), if you're really lucky.

There are several indoor shopping options, including the showpiece Victoria Square shopping centre and the older CastleCourt Shopping Centre (see page 22), where you'll find everything you need to keep you fed, watered and clothed for the day.

If the rain carries on into the evening, take in a film at the Queen's Film Theatre (see page 98), classical music at the Waterfront Hall (see page 67) or performing arts at the Crescent Arts Centre (see page 97). Of course, you could also take refuge in one of the city's many public houses, where the company's so convivial that you might be tempted to knock out a quick rain dance to keep the party going.

CastleCourt shopping centre: no umbrella needed

On arrival

TIME DIFFERENCE

Belfast follows Greenwich Mean Time (GMT). During Daylight Saving Time (last Sunday in March to last Sunday in October), the clocks are put ahead 1 hour – British Summer Time (BST).

ARRIVING

By air

Belfast has two airports: Belfast International Airport and George Best Belfast City Airport. The international airport is located 13 km (8 miles) northwest of the city and is Northern Ireland's busiest airport. Facilities include shops and restaurants, bureaux de change, postal services, cash machines, airport information, Business Lounge and baby changing facilities.

The blue and white Airport Express 300 bus operates between the airport and Belfast every 10–20 minutes and leaves from the bus stop opposite the terminal exit. The bus stops at Laganside Buscentre and Europa Buscentre (approximate journey time 30–40 minutes, depending on traffic). There are also approved taxis available outside the terminal.

George Best Belfast City Airport is between Belfast and Holywood, 8 km (5 miles) from the city centre. There are two shops and a range of restaurants/snack bars, as well as cash dispensers, bureaux de change and wireless Internet access.

A shuttle bus operates between the airport and Sydenham railway station. Translink operates a twice-hourly rail service to Belfast Central, Botanic and Great Victoria Street stations (journey time up to 15 minutes). Flexibus operates the Airport Express

The City Airport bus

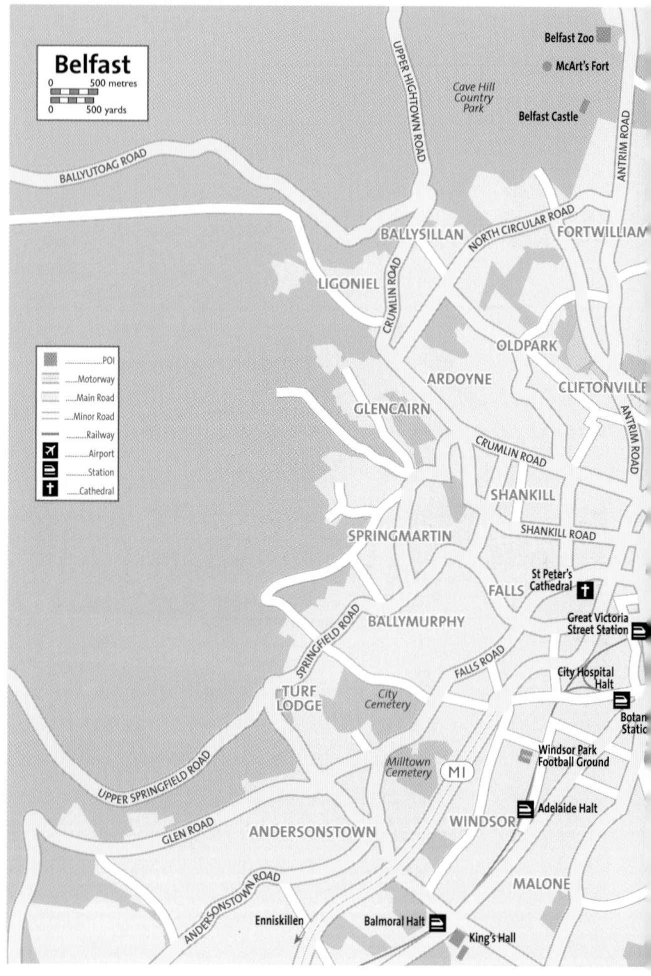

Belfast
0 500 metres
0 500 yards
POI
Motorway
Main Road
Minor Road
Railway
Airport
Station
Cathedral
Belfast Zoo
McArt's Fort
Cave Hill Country Park
Belfast Castle
UPPER HIGHTOWN ROAD
ANTRIM ROAD
BALLYUTOAG ROAD
BALLYSILLAN
NORTH CIRCULAR ROAD
FORTWILLIAM
LIGONIEL
CRUMLIN ROAD
OLDPARK
ARDOYNE
CLIFTONVILLE
GLENCAIRN
CRUMLIN ROAD
ANTRIM ROAD
SHANKILL
SPRINGMARTIN
SHANKILL ROAD
St Peter's Cathedral
FALLS
BALLYMURPHY
Great Victoria Street Station
SPRINGFIELD ROAD
FALLS ROAD
City Hospital Halt
TURF LODGE
City Cemetery
Milltown Cemetery
M1
Windsor Park Football Ground
UPPER SPRINGFIELD ROAD
Adelaide Halt
WINDSOR
GLEN ROAD
ANDERSONSTOWN
MALONE
ANDERSONSTOWN ROAD
Enniskillen
Balmoral Halt
King's Hall

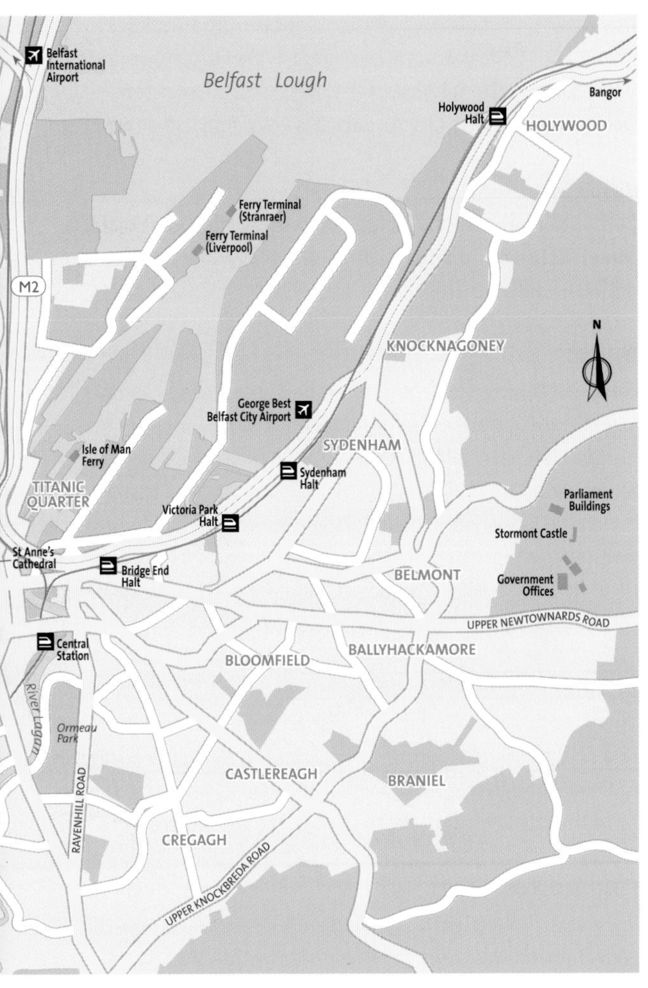

Belfast International Airport
Belfast Lough
Bangor
Holywood Halt
HOLYWOOD
Ferry Terminal (Stranraer)
Ferry Terminal (Liverpool)
M2
N
KNOCKNAGONEY
George Best Belfast City Airport
SYDENHAM
Isle of Man Ferry
Sydenham Halt
TITANIC QUARTER
Parliament Buildings
Victoria Park Halt
Stormont Castle
St Anne's Cathedral
Bridge End Halt
BELMONT
Government Offices
UPPER NEWTOWNARDS ROAD
Central Station
BALLYHACKAMORE
BLOOMFIELD
River Lagan
Ormeau Park
CASTLEREAGH
BRANIEL
RAVENHILL ROAD
CREGAGH
UPPER KNOCKBREDA ROAD

bus service (route 600) every 20 minutes from the airport terminal to Belfast Europa Buscentre, which takes 13 minutes.

Belfast International Airport Ⓦ www.belfastairport.com

George Best Belfast City Airport Ⓦ www.belfastcityairport.com

By rail

Belfast railway stations include **Belfast Central**, **Great Victoria Street**, **Botanic** and **City Hospital** (see Ⓦ www.translink.co.uk for details of all).

By road

Long-distance buses arrive at **Europa Buscentre** (ⓐ Glengall Street), which leads on to Great Victoria Street, next to the Europa Hotel and just a few minutes' walk from Donegall Square and City Hall.

Visitors arriving by car at Belfast ferry port should follow signs for the A2, Bangor or Belfast city centre. From Larne ferry port, head for the A8, then M2 and A2. From the north and northwest, you'll arrive via the M2, from the south via the M1 or A1.

By water

There is a ferry port in Belfast, close to the city centre. It moved to a new terminal building 3.2 km (2 miles) along the north side of Belfast Lough in 2008, so you'll need to take bus number 96 from the city centre to Westbank Road or get a taxi.

FINDING YOUR FEET

Visitors to Belfast will be greeted with a warm Northern Irish welcome and the locals are keen to show that the city has a lot to offer. People are generally easy-going and it won't be difficult to quickly immerse yourself in the *craic* (good time). It isn't a large city, so even if you wander down a side street in the city centre, it won't be long before you find your way back to a main road. If you do get lost, just ask for directions – you'll find that people are willing to help.

ORIENTATION

Belfast city centre is bound by the Westlink (which links the M2 and the M1) to the north and west, by the M2 and River Lagan to the east, and Shaftesbury Square to the south. At the heart of the city centre is Donegall Square, with the landmark City Hall (see pages 63–4) at its centre. North of Donegall Square are the main shopping streets of Donegall Place, Royal Avenue, High Street and Cornmarket and the oldest parts of the city. The Cathedral Quarter is located at the northern end of the city centre around Donegall Street. Heading east, High Street crosses Victoria Street and leads to the Albert Clock, Custom House Square and the River Lagan. Heading south along the river are the Lagan Lookout, Waterfront Hall (see page 67) and Central Station.

GETTING AROUND

Visitors can easily walk around the city centre on foot, and even south to the Ulster Museum (see page 98), west along Falls and Shankill roads, or along the riverfront. However, for longer distances or if you're tired, there is an efficient urban bus service called the Metro, with main departure points in Donegall Square and Wellington Place. You can buy Metro day tickets,

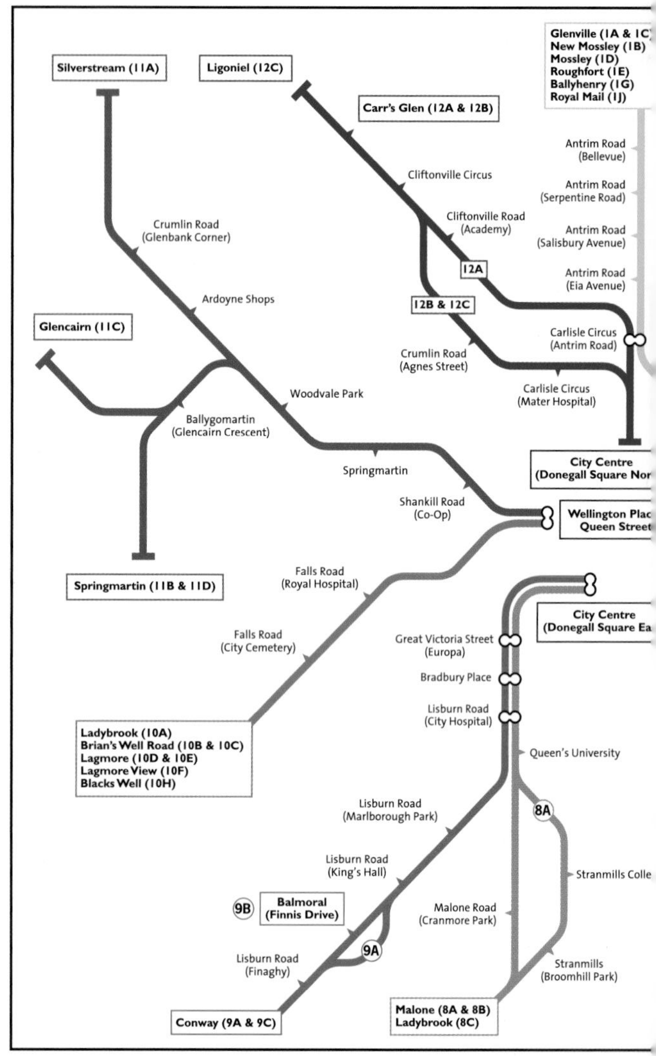

Silverstream (11A)
Ligoniel (12C)
Carr's Glen (12A & 12B)
Glenville (1A & 1C
New Mossley (1B)
Mossley (1D)
Roughfort (1E)
Ballyhenry (1G)
Royal Mail (1J)
Antrim Road (Bellevue)
Cliftonville Circus
Antrim Road (Serpentine Road)
Crumlin Road (Glenbank Corner)
Cliftonville Road (Academy)
Antrim Road (Salisbury Avenue)
12A
Antrim Road (Eia Avenue)
Ardoyne Shops
12B & 12C
Glencairn (11C)
Carlisle Circus (Antrim Road)
Crumlin Road (Agnes Street)
Carlisle Circus (Mater Hospital)
Woodvale Park
Ballygomartin (Glencairn Crescent)
City Centre (Donegall Square Nor
Springmartin
Shankill Road (Co-Op)
Wellington Plac
Queen Street
Falls Road (Royal Hospital)
Springmartin (11B & 11D)
City Centre (Donegall Square Ea
Falls Road (City Cemetery)
Great Victoria Street (Europa)
Bradbury Place
Lisburn Road (City Hospital)
Ladybrook (10A)
Brian's Well Road (10B & 10C)
Lagmore (10D & 10E)
Lagmore View (10F)
Blacks Well (10H)
Queen's University
Lisburn Road (Marlborough Park)
8A
Lisburn Road (King's Hall)
Stranmills Colle
9B
Balmoral (Finnis Drive)
Malone Road (Cranmore Park)
9A
Lisburn Road (Finaghy)
Stranmills (Broomhill Park)
Conway (9A & 9C)
Malone (8A & 8B)
Ladybrook (8C)

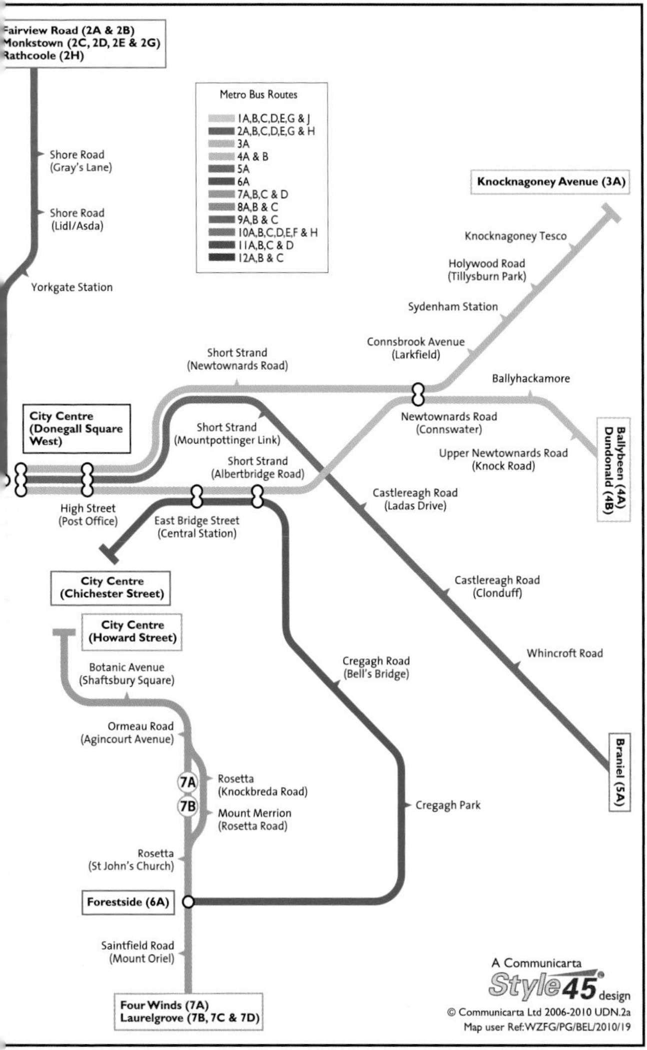

Fairview Road (2A & 2B)
Monkstown (2C, 2D, 2E & 2G)
Rathcoole (2H)
Metro Bus Routes
1A,B,C,D,E,G & J
2A,B,C,D,E,G & H
3A
4A & B
5A
6A
7A,B,C & D
8A,B & C
9A,B & C
10A,B,C,D,E,F & H
11A,B,C & D
12A,B & C
Shore Road (Gray's Lane)
Shore Road (Lidl/Asda)
Yorkgate Station
Knocknagoney Avenue (3A)
Knocknagoney Tesco
Holywood Road (Tillysburn Park)
Sydenham Station
Connsbrook Avenue (Larkfield)
Short Strand (Newtownards Road)
Ballyhackamore
City Centre (Donegall Square West)
Short Strand (Mountpottinger Link)
Newtownards Road (Connswater)
Upper Newtownards Road (Knock Road)
Ballybeen (4A)
Dundonald (4B)
Short Strand (Albertbridge Road)
Castlereagh Road (Ladas Drive)
High Street (Post Office)
East Bridge Street (Central Station)
City Centre (Chichester Street)
Castlereagh Road (Clonduff)
City Centre (Howard Street)
Whincroft Road
Botanic Avenue (Shaftsbury Square)
Cregagh Road (Bell's Bridge)
Ormeau Road (Agincourt Avenue)
Braniel (5A)
7A
Rosetta (Knockbreda Road)
7B
Mount Merrion (Rosetta Road)
Cregagh Park
Rosetta (St John's Church)
Forestside (6A)
Saintfield Road (Mount Oriel)
Four Winds (7A)
Laurelgrove (7B, 7C & 7D)
A Communicarta Style45 design
© Communicarta Ltd 2006-2010 UDN.2a
Map user Ref: WZFG/PG/BEL/2010/19

giving you the freedom to hop on and off buses as you please. You can buy these from the driver or from the Metro Ticket and Information kiosk in Donegall Square West.

Alternatively, there are shared black taxis that charge a similar rate to buses, operating from Bedford Street (off High Street) to the Shankill Road, or from the car park on the corner of Castle Street and King Street. To get further afield, buses from Laganside Buscentre go to North Down, while Europa Buscentre serves the rest of the province, Dublin and international destinations.

CAR HIRE

If you're only planning on staying in Belfast, you don't really need to hire a car. However, if you want to get around outside the city as you please, then car hire is available at both Belfast International Airport and George Best Belfast City Airport:

Argus ⓣ 0870 625 1234 ⓦ www.arguscarhire.com
Avis ⓣ International Airport 0844 544 6028, City Airport 0844 544 6036 ⓦ www.avis.co.uk
Budget ⓣ International Airport 0233 442 3332, City Airport 0844 544 6036 ⓦ www.budget.ie
Europcar ⓣ International & City Airports 028 9045 0904 ⓦ www.europcar.co.uk
Hertz ⓣ International Airport 028 944 22533, City Airport 028 9073 2541 ⓦ www.hertz.co.uk
National Car Rental ⓣ International & City Airports 028 9442 2285 ⓦ www.nationalcar.co.uk

City Hall

THE CITY OF Belfast

City centre

The oldest part of Belfast is High Street and Castle Place, where the city's first castle once stood. Off here you'll discover various 'entries', side alleys with historic pubs and bars hidden away, and at the end the iconic Albert Memorial Clock. Just north of here is the artsy Cathedral Quarter, around Donegall Street, with St Anne's Cathedral at its centre. Today, the heart of the city has shifted south to Donegall Square, where City Hall marks Belfast's city status.

SIGHTS & ATTRACTIONS

Albert Memorial Clock

Built between 1865 and 1870 as a memorial to Queen Victoria's late consort, the Albert Memorial Clock is now one of the city's primary landmarks, partly because of its distinctive lean of around 1.4 m (4½ ft), blamed on the fact that it was built on reclaimed land. Constructed from sandstone, and standing over 34 m (111 ft) high, the clock has a life-size statue of Prince Albert on the west side and a 2-tonne bell. ⓐ Queen's Square
Bus: Laganside Buscentre

Belfast Citysightseeing bus tour

The quickest way to get a flavour of the city, buses leave at regular intervals from Castle Place and follow a circular route that takes in Belfast city centre, Cathedral Quarter, Titanic Quarter, Stormont, Laganside, Crumlin Road Courthouse and Gaol, Shankill Road, Peace Line, Falls Road, University District

The Albert Memorial Clock

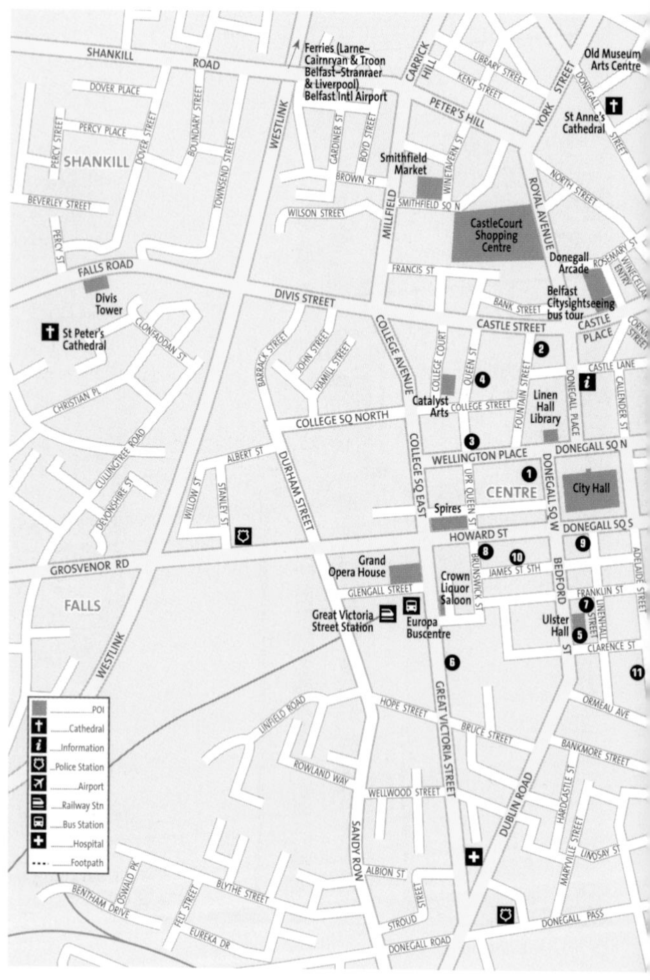

SHANKILL ROAD
DOVER PLACE
PERCY PLACE
PERCY STREET
DOVER STREET
BOUNDARY STREET
TOWNSEND STREET
WESTLINK
SHANKILL
BEVERLEY STREET
PERCY ST
FALLS ROAD
Divis Tower
St Peter's Cathedral
CLONFADDAN ST
CHRISTIAN PL
CULLINGTREE ROAD
DEVONSHIRE ST
GROSVENOR RD
FALLS
WESTLINK
Ferries (Larne–Cairnryan & Troon Belfast–Stranraer & Liverpool) Belfast Intl Airport
GARDINER ST
BOYD STREET
BROWN ST
WILSON STREET
MILLFIELD
Smithfield Market
SMITHFIELD SQ N
CARRICK HILL
LIBRARY STREET
KENT STREET
PETER'S HILL
WINETAVERN ST
YORK STREET
ROYAL AVENUE
NORTH STREET
DONEGALL STREET
Old Museum Arts Centre
St Anne's Cathedral
CastleCourt Shopping Centre
FRANCIS ST
DIVIS STREET
BANK STREET
Donegall Arcade
ROSEMARY ST
WINECELLAR ENTRY
Belfast Citysightseeing bus tour
CASTLE STREET
CASTLE PLACE
CORN MARKET STREET
BARRACK STREET
JOHN STREET
HAMILL STREET
COLLEGE AVENUE
COLLEGE COURT
QUEEN ST
FOUNTAIN STREET
DONEGALL PLACE
CASTLE LANE
CALLENDER ST
Catalyst Arts
COLLEGE STREET
Linen Hall Library
COLLEGE SQ NORTH
WELLINGTON PLACE
DONEGALL SQ N
ALBERT ST
WILLOW ST
STANLEY ST
DURHAM STREET
COLLEGE SQ EAST
UPR QUEEN ST
CENTRE
DONEGALL SQ W
City Hall
Spires
DONEGALL SQ S
HOWARD ST
Grand Opera House
BRUNSWICK ST
JAMES ST STH
BEDFORD ST
ADELAIDE STREET
GLENGALL STREET
Crown Liquor Saloon
FRANKLIN ST
Great Victoria Street Station
Europa Buscentre
Ulster Hall
LINENHALL STREET
CLARENCE ST
ORMEAU AVE
HOPE STREET
BRUCE STREET
GREAT VICTORIA STREET
LINFIELD ROAD
ROWLAND WAY
WELLWOOD STREET
BANKMORE STREET
DUBLIN ROAD
HARDCASTLE ST
MARYVILLE STREET
LINDSAY ST
SANDY ROW
ALBION ST
BLYTHE STREET
OSWALD PK
BENTHAM DRIVE
FELT STREET
EUREKA DR
STROUD STREET
DONEGALL ROAD
DONEGALL PASS
POI
Cathedral
Information
Police Station
Airport
Railway Stn
Bus Station
Hospital
Footpath

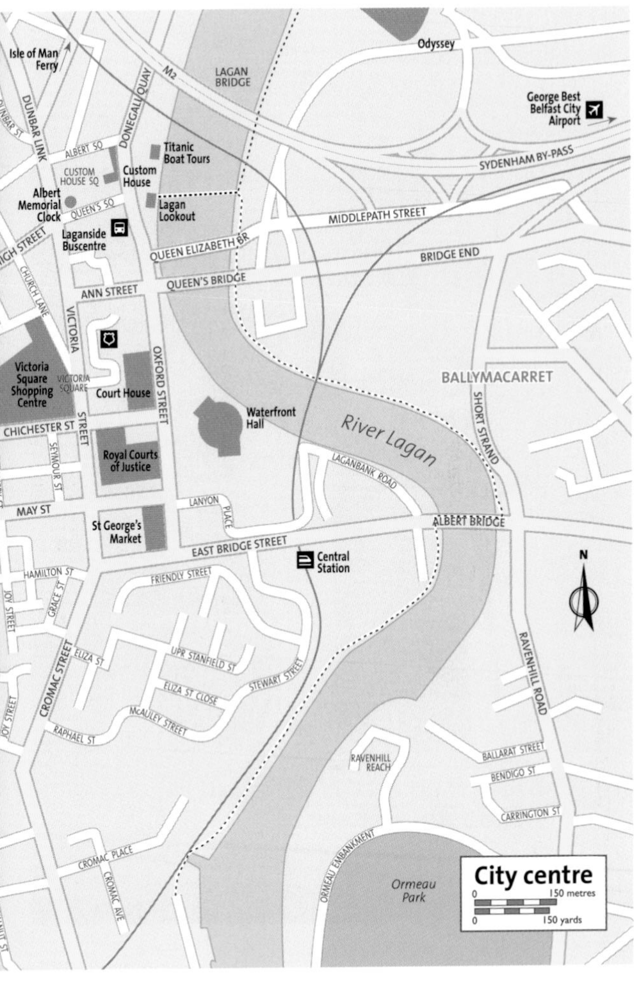
Isle of Man Ferry
Odyssey
LAGAN BRIDGE
M2
George Best Belfast City Airport
DUNBAR LINK
DUNBAR ST
DONEGALL QUAY
ALBERT SQ
CUSTOM HOUSE SQ
Titanic Boat Tours
Custom House
SYDENHAM BY-PASS
Albert Memorial Clock
QUEEN'S SQ
Lagan Lookout
MIDDLEPATH STREET
HIGH STREET
Laganside Buscentre
QUEEN ELIZABETH BR
BRIDGE END
CHURCH LANE
ANN STREET
QUEEN'S BRIDGE
VICTORIA STREET
Victoria Square Shopping Centre
VICTORIA SQUARE
Court House
OXFORD STREET
BALLYMACARRET
Waterfront Hall
SHORT STRAND
CHICHESTER ST
River Lagan
SEYMOUR ST
Royal Courts of Justice
LAGANBANK ROAD
MAY ST
LANYON PLACE
ALBERT BRIDGE
St George's Market
EAST BRIDGE STREET
Central Station
N
HAMILTON ST
FRIENDLY STREET
JOY STREET
GRACE ST
CROMAC STREET
ELIZA ST
UPR STANFIELD ST
RAVENHILL ROAD
STEWART STREET
ELIZA ST CLOSE
McAULEY STREET
RAPHAEL ST
RAVENHILL REACH
BALLARAT STREET
BENDIGO ST
CARRINGTON ST
ORMEAU EMBANKMENT
CROMAC PLACE
CROMAC AVE
Ormeau Park
City centre
0
150 metres
0
150 yards

Belfast Cathedral

and Botanic nightlife areas. You're given a route map on the bus and there is a live commentary by a local guide on the way. You can hop on and off en route. ⓐ High Street ⓣ 028 9077 0990 ⓦ www.belfastcitysightseeing.com ⓛ 10.00–16.30 daily (Sept–May can close early depending on demand) ⓑ Bus: Royal Avenue, Donegall Square ⓘ Admission charge

Cathedral Quarter

One of the oldest city districts, the Cathedral Quarter had become quite rundown, but it's now seeing something of a renaissance. The main focal point is St Anne's Cathedral (see page 65) on Donegall Street and the roads and alleys around it. A favourite with artists and musicians, theatre groups and dance studios due to the low rents, it is fast becoming a trendy arts/media area with new companies moving in and restorations taking place. Look out for the Duke of York pub (see page 72), the original premises of the Northern Bank, and don't miss Irish News, News Letter or the various community arts centres and galleries.
ⓐ Donegall Street ⓑ Bus: Royal Avenue

City Hall

Built in the Edwardian Baroque style – and, indeed, thought to be the finest example of that genre – and opened in 1906, City Hall stands on the site of the old White Linen Hall. Plans for the building began after Queen Victoria, in a fit of generosity, gave Belfast city status in 1888, in recognition of the contribution that its residents' blood, sweat and tears made to the Empire's coffers. There was clearly no great rush to get things moving, however, as construction only began ten years later under the magnificently named architect Sir Alfred Brumwell Thomas. Highlights include the emphatic grand entrance, the main dome with its whispering gallery, grand staircase and the mural by Belfast artist John Luke. City Hall is one of Belfast's leading chill-out locations. The ample grounds are popular with office workers who want to enjoy their lunch break in the sun. The front gates meanwhile are a major hangout for goths, emos, bikers and anyone else looking for a meeting place and a natter. ⓐ Donegall Square ⓣ 028 9032 0202, minicom 028 9027 0405 ⓦ www.belfastcity.gov.uk ⓛ 09.00–17.00 Mon–Fri (tours 11.00, 14.00 & 15.00 Mon–Fri, 14.00 & 15.00 Sat) ⓝ Bus: Donegall Square

Crown Liquor Saloon

A popular venue with locals and tourists, this is a fine example of a Victorian public house or 'gin palace', now owned by the National Trust. The outside is clad in colourful tiles, while the inside is a rich mix of carved wooden snugs, red granite-top bars, mosaics, tiles, mirrors and columns. ⓐ 46 Great Victoria Street ⓣ 028 9024 3187 ⓦ www.crownbar.com ⓝ Bus: Europa Buscentre, Donegall Square

Custom House Square

Renovated a few years ago to highlight its original use as a speakers' corner, the paved square now has a bronze statue of 'The Speaker' and large copper-based lights along its edge representing 'The Hecklers'. The historic Calder Fountain was also restored, and lights follow the course of the underground River Farset (which runs the length of High Street). The square is now used for concerts,

A RIGHT ROYAL MONIKER

An old Belfast story has it that the name of the Crown Liquor Saloon was chosen by the Protestant wife of the landlord to show her allegiance to the British monarchy. Her husband, a Catholic, wasn't keen on this idea, and only agreed if he could put a mosaic of a crown in the doorway – that way everyone would have to step on it as they walked in to the pub. The mosaic, together with the Crown's celebrated Victorian snugs (complete with antique bells for getting the attention of the bar staff), is still there to greet visitors today.

festivals and other events, as well as being a favourite hangout for skateboarders. The central focus of the square is the mid-19th-century **Custom House**, one of the few remaining custom houses in the UK still occupied by Her Majesty's Revenue and Customs Officers. It is open to the public on European Heritage Open Days only. ⓐ Custom House Square Ⓡ Bus: Laganside Buscentre

St Anne's Cathedral

Also known as the Cathedral Church of St Anne (or simply Belfast Cathedral), this was Belfast's first Church of Ireland parish. The foundation stone was laid in 1899 but it wasn't completed until 1981. In 2007 a new modern, stainless-steel spire was erected, which towers above the cathedral and is lit up at night. ⓐ Lower Donegall Street ⓣ 028 9032 8332 ⓦ www.belfastcathedral.org ⓛ 10.00–16.00 Mon–Sat Ⓡ Bus: Royal Avenue

CULTURE

Catalyst Arts

One of the city's fringe arts centres, this artist-run venue supports innovative projects in art, film, photography, music and literature. ⓐ 2nd Floor, 5 College Court ⓣ 028 9031 3303 ⓦ www.catalystarts.org.uk ⓔ info@catalystarts.org.uk ◷ Performance times vary – check website for details Ⓝ Bus: Donegall Square/Royal Avenue ❗ Admission charge

Grand Opera House

You're unlikely to see opera at this historic venue but you can catch off-West End theatre, musicals and pantomimes. The renovated opera house now has an extension that has added an all-day café/bistro, bars and more wheelchair space and access. ⓐ Great Victoria Street ⓣ 028 9024 1919 ⓦ www.goh.co.uk ◷ Various Ⓝ Bus: Europa Buscentre/Donegall Square

Linen Hall Library

Founded in 1788, the Linen Hall contains the best Irish and Local Studies Collection of books covering everything from early Belfast and Ulster to the contemporary NI Political Collection on the Troubles. A centre of cultural and creative life, it hosts a varied programme of exhibitions, readings, discussion groups and lectures. Use the library for reference or read a few of your favourite newspapers. ⓐ 17 Donegall Square North ⓣ 028 9032 1707 ⓦ www.linenhall.com ◷ 09.30–17.30 Mon–Fri, 09.30–16.00 Sat; closed for one week in July, check website for details Ⓝ Bus: Donegall Square

Old Museum Arts Centre

Presents contemporary theatre, music, dance and visual art from Northern Ireland and overseas. A state of-the-art replacement is due to open in the Cathedral Quarter in 2011. ⓐ 7 St Anne's Square ⓣ 028 9023 5053 ⓦ www.oldmuseumartscentre.org ⓛ Performance times vary – check website for details ⓝ Donegall Square ⓘ Admission charge

Ulster Hall

Reopened in 2009 following an £8.5 million renovation, the Ulster Hall is one of the city's premier venues for classical concerts, jazz and popular music. ⓐ Bedford Street ⓣ 028 9032 3900 ⓦ www.ulsterhall.co.uk ⓛ Performance times vary – check website for details ⓝ Bus: Donegall Square

Waterfront Hall

The city's major concert and conference venue. ⓐ 2 Lanyon Place ⓣ 028 9033 4455 ⓦ www.waterfront.co.uk ⓛ Performance times vary – check website for details ⓝ Bus: Laganside Buscentre ⓘ Admission charge

RETAIL THERAPY

The hub of Belfast's shopping is around Donegall Place and Royal Avenue, where you'll find high-street stores and the large CastleCourt shopping centre (see page 22). More shops can be found along High Street and Cornmarket, which leads to Belfast's new showpiece Victoria Square shopping centre (see page 22). Home to high-street and designer stores, it also boasts several

MARKETS

The main market in Belfast city centre is **St George's Market** on Oxford Street/May Street. It's a late 19th-century market that's had a makeover, buffing up its Victorian splendour. On Friday there's a vibrant mixed market (🕒 06.00–14.00) and on Saturday live music and food at the City Food & Garden Market (🕒 10.00–15.00). Catch the free market bus on market days from Donegall Place or Castle Place. **Smithfield Market** was once a thriving market but the old Victorian building was sadly demolished in 1974. After years of prefabricated units, a new market building opened in 1986. It's not as trendy as St George's but sells a little of everything and is useful for products and trades no longer found on the high street, including leather workers, a seamstress and martial arts products (🕒 09.00–17.00 Mon–Sat).

restaurants, a cinema and a glass dome with a viewing platform. Donegall Arcade (see page 22) is another small shopping centre.

TAKING A BREAK

Apartment £ ❶ Trendy café-bar-restaurant with panini and pasta downstairs and Asian-fusion dining upstairs; and then there are the views of City Hall. ⓐ 2 Donegall Square West ⓣ 028 9050 9777 ⓦ www.apartmentbelfast.com 🕒 09.00–01.00 (last food orders 21.00, 22.00 Thur) Mon–Sat, 12.00–01.00 (last food orders 20.00) Sun

La Boca £ ❷ An Argentine restaurant in Belfast, no less (and an art gallery too). Top dishes to try in this chic and friendly eatery are portobello mushrooms stuffed with Serrano ham, Manchego and parmesan cheese, and beef and olive empanadas. The wine list is fabulous. ⓐ 6 Fountain Street ⓣ 028 9032 3087 ⓦ www.labocabelfast.com ◷ 10.30–15.00 Mon, 10.30–19.00 Tues, 10.30–21.00 Wed & Thur, 10.30–22.00 Fri & Sat, closed Sun

Grüb £ ❸ One of the city's newest eateries, Grüb has a whole counter of soup options, as well as fresh filled bagels and sandwiches, wraps and salads. Grab one straight from the fridge

Hit St George's Market at dawn on Friday

or wait while they're made to order. ⓐ 13 Wellington Place ⓣ 028 9034 4925 ◷ 07.00–17.00 Mon–Fri, 09.00–17.00 Sat, closed Sun

Café Renoir £ ❹ Try home-made scones, fresh bread and organic jams from the Loney family farm. There's a second branch along Botanic that has a mixed menu of breakfast, pizza and Asian dishes, and a counter full of tempting cakes. ⓐ 5–7 Queen Street ⓣ 028 9032 5592 ◷ 09.00–17.00 Mon–Sat (until 19.30 Thur)

Deanes Deli ££ ❺ Michelin-star chef Michael Deane's New York-style deli with olives, charcuterie boards, burgers, salads and soup for lunch, and steaks and fish and chips in the evening. The adjacent store sells Deane's branded products. ⓐ 44 Bedford Street ⓣ 028 9024 8800 ⓦ www.michaeldeane.co.uk ◷ 12.00–15.00 & 17.00–21.00 Mon & Tues, 12.00–15.00 & 17.00–22.00 Wed–Sat

AFTER DARK

RESTAURANTS

The Red Panda £ ❻ Renowned Chinese restaurant in the Golden Mile. ⓐ 60 Great Victoria Street ⓣ 028 9080 8700 ◷ 12.00–15.00 & 17.00–23.30 Mon–Fri, 16.00–23.30 Sat, 13.30–22.30 Sun

Coco ££ ❼ One of the most recent additions to Belfast's dining scene, Coco has an eclectic look of wooden floors, wild wallpaper and contemporary prints. Lunches include Portavogie prawns and curry-spiced fish and chips, while dinner offers mains of seared sole and honey-roast pork belly. ⓐ 7–11 Linenhall Street ⓣ 028 9031 1150 ⓦ http://cocobelfast.com ◷ 12.00–15.00 Mon–Fri, 18.00–23.00 Sat, 12.00–16.00 Sun

Deanes ££ ❽ Sophisticated brasserie where you can treat yourself to dishes such as free-range Fermanagh chicken, Lough Erne beef or fish of the day. ⓐ 36–40 Howard Street ⓣ 028 9033 1134 ⓕ 028 9056 0001 ⓦ www.michaeldeane.co.uk ◷ 12.00–15.00 & 18.00–22.00 Mon–Sat

The Grill Room & Bar ££ ❾ Stop for a cocktail or two, and maybe a speciality burger, and hear the house band every Wed, Thur and Sun. ⓐ Ten Square Hotel, 10 Donegall Square South ⓣ 028 9024 1001 ⓦ www.tensquare.co.uk ◷ 07.00–10.00 & 12.00–22.00 Mon–Fri, 08.00–10.30 & 12.00–22.00 Sat, 08.00–13.00 Sun

James Street South ££ ❿ European cuisine in contemporary surroundings with set lunch and pre-theatre menus. In 2010 chef-owner Niall McKenna won the Northern Ireland round of the BBC's *Great British Menu* and was selected to make dessert for a royal banquet. ⓐ 21 James Street South ⓣ 028 9043 4310 ⓦ www.jamesstreetsouth.co.uk ◷ 12.00–14.45 & 17.45–22.45 Mon–Sat, 17.30–21.00 Sun

Zen Restaurant £££ ⓫ Excellent Japanese restaurant serving sushi, sashimi and fusion food. ⓐ 55–59 Adelaide Street ⓣ 028 9023 2244 ◷ 12.00–15.00 & 17.00–23.30 Mon–Fri, 18.00–01.00 Sat, 13.30–22.00 Sun

PUBS & CLUBS

Café Vaudeville A former bank that was transformed into one of the city's glitziest bars. A few years after opening, it's as popular as ever, with its extravagant mix of high ceilings, chandeliers and gilt-framed pictures. Stop for coffee, tea, modern European food, beers and cocktails. ⓐ 25–39 Arthur Street ⓣ 028 9043 9160 ⓦ www.cafevaudeville.com ◷ 11.30–01.00 Mon–Sat

Crown Liquor Saloon A drink in this historic Belfast pub is a must. Sit in a snug or at the bar with a pint, or have a spot of lunch in the Crown Dining Rooms upstairs, which features local specialities like sausage and champ. ⓐ 46 Great Victoria Street ⓣ 028 9027 9901 ⓦ www.crownbar.com ◷ 11.30–23.00 Mon–Sat, 12.30–22.00 Sun

Duke of York One of the oldest pubs in the city, in its heyday it was frequented by the literati, politicians and hacks who worked in the nearby newspaper industry. Sit in a snug and enjoy a few pints and traditional Irish food. ⓐ Commercial Court, off Donegall Street, Cathedral Quarter ⓣ 028 9024 1062 ◷ 11.30–23.00 Mon, 11.30–01.00 Tues–Sun

The John Hewitt A popular venue, owned by the Belfast Unemployed Resource Centre. The bar has a good reputation for traditional music every night of the week except Weds; frequented by local artists, writers and journalists. ⓐ 51 Donegall Street ⓣ 028 9023 3768 ⓦ www.thejohnhewitt.com ◷ 11.30–01.00 Mon–Fri, 12.00–01.00 Sat, doesn't always open on Sun

The Limelight/Spring & Airbrake/Katy Daly's Three venues in one. Katy Daly's is a good place for cheap eats, and The Limelight is Belfast's best live music venue, closely followed by Spring & Airbrake. In addition to big-name bands, they host an array of entertainments, including open mic nights, gay discos, DJ sets and stand-up comedy. ⓐ 15–17 Ormeau Avenue ⓣ 028 9032 7007 ⓦ www.cdcleisure.net ⓛ Varies

Mynt Formerly Parliament, this was Belfast's first gay bar and is still its biggest with a lounge bar and two club rooms with more in the pipeline. You can eat international food here, stop for a drink or stay for karaoke nights, game shows and occasional live music. ⓐ 2–16 Dunbar Street ⓣ 028 9023 4520 ⓦ www.myntbelfast.com ⓛ 12.00–23.30 Mon & Tues, 12.00–00.30 Wed, 12.00–02.00 Thur, 12.00–05.00 Fri, 12.00–06.00 Sat, 12.00–03.00 Sun

Robinson's Bars Five distinct venues under one roof. Take your pick from the saloon bar, Fibber Magee's in the back with live traditional music, BT1, a stylish basement chill-out bar, the sophisticated first-floor Bistro and, finally, the chic Roxy nightclub. ⓐ 38–42 Great Victoria Street ⓣ 028 9024 7447 ⓦ www.robinsonsbar.co.uk ⓛ 11.30–01.00 Mon–Sat, 12.30–24.00 Sun

White's Tavern Claims to be the oldest pub in Belfast, just off High Street. Home-made food is served during the day and there are live bands every Fri, Sat and Sun night. ⓐ 2–4 Winecellar Entry ⓣ 028 9024 3080 ⓦ www.whitestavern.co.uk ⓛ 11.30–23.00 daily

North & West Belfast

The Falls and Shankill roads are among the most notorious in Belfast, a hotspot for nationalist and loyalist clashes during the Troubles, but these areas had been divided along religious lines way before the recent conflict. When migrants poured into Belfast during the Industrial Revolution they flocked to areas that were already either Catholic or Protestant, bringing their rivalries with them. The Shankill Road, which stands between West Belfast and North Belfast, was actually the site of settlements dating back to the Stone Age, but its name derives from the Gaelic *Sean Cill*, meaning 'old church'. Today, there's nothing Gaelic about the Shankill, and despite the official end of the armed struggle, it remains rundown, struggling to rebuild its community, displaying its identity through murals and flags. Tourists are attracted here to see the murals and the peace line that divides it from the Catholic Falls Road. A symbol of Republican West Belfast, the Falls Road was extremely deprived, maybe even more so in the 1960s, but today it is celebrating its Irishness with Irish names, Celtic script on signs and Irish cultural centres and sports. You should visit the murals in both areas to begin to understand the origins and impact of the conflict. In general, most visitors prefer to eat, drink and stay in the city centre or South Belfast, but the locals are encouraging tourism by opening their own B&Bs. Overlooking West Belfast, the hills of Cave Hill Country Park are a must-see, with Belfast Castle, its visitor centre and trails to McArt's Fort providing an insight into the city's history. Nearby, Belfast Zoo provides light relief for children.

SIGHTS & ATTRACTIONS

Belfast Castle

The original Belfast Castle was built by the Normans in the 12th century in what is now the city centre (Castle Street). Another castle followed on the same site, but this was burned down in the early 18th century, and it was the Marquis of Donegall who commissioned the current building on the slopes of Cave Hill. Belfast Castle was finished in 1870 and presented to the City of Belfast in 1934. It has been a popular location for weddings, dances and afternoon teas ever since. You can visit the castle but access depends on what events are taking place. There is also a shop and restaurant, as well as a visitor centre on the

Cave Hill Country Park overlooks the city

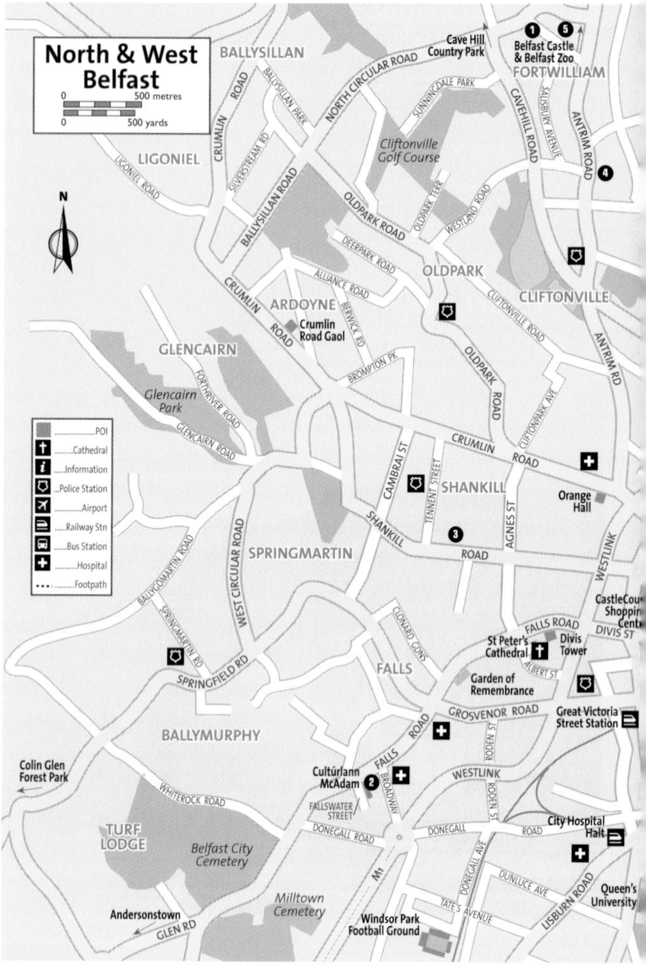

North & West Belfast

0 500 metres
0 500 yards

N

	POI
✝	Cathedral
i	Information
	Police Station
	Airport
	Railway Stn
	Bus Station
✚	Hospital
----	Footpath

BALLYSILLAN
Cave Hill Country Park
❶ ❺ Belfast Castle & Belfast Zoo
FORTWILLIAM
NORTH CIRCULAR ROAD
SUNNINGDALE PARK
BALLYSILLAN PARK
CRUMLIN ROAD
CAVEHILL ROAD
SALISBURY AVENUE
ANTRIM ROAD
❹
LIGONIEL
LIGONIEL ROAD
SILVERSTREAM RD
BALLYSILLAN ROAD
Cliftonville Golf Course
OLDPARK ROAD
OLDPARK TERR
WESTLAND ROAD
DEERPARK ROAD
OLDPARK
CLIFTONVILLE
ALLIANCE ROAD
CRUMLIN ROAD
ARDOYNE
Crumlin Road Gaol
BERWICK RD
CLIFTONVILLE ROAD
OLDPARK ROAD
ANTRIM RD
GLENCAIRN
FORTHRIVER ROAD
BROMPTON PK
Glencairn Park
GLENCAIRN ROAD
CLIFTONPARK AVE
CRUMLIN ROAD
CAMBRAI ST
TENNENT STREET
SHANKILL
AGNES ST
Orange Hall
SHANKILL ROAD
❸
WESTLINK
BALLYGOMARTIN ROAD
WEST CIRCULAR ROAD
SPRINGMARTIN
CastleCourt Shopping Centre
DIVIS ST
SPRINGMARTIN RD
CLONARD GDNS
FALLS ROAD
St Peter's Cathedral
Divis Tower
ALBERT ST
SPRINGFIELD RD
FALLS
Garden of Remembrance
GROSVENOR ROAD
Great Victoria Street Station
BALLYMURPHY
RODEN ST
Colin Glen Forest Park
FALLS ROAD
Cultúrlann McAdam ❷
BROADWAY
WESTLINK
WHITEROCK ROAD
FALLSWATER STREET
RODEN ST
DONEGALL ROAD
DONEGALL ROAD
City Hospital Halt
TURF LODGE
Belfast City Cemetery
M1
DONEGALL AVE
DUNLUCE AVE
Milltown Cemetery
TATE'S AVENUE
LISBURN ROAD
Queen's University
Andersonstown
GLEN RD
Windsor Park Football Ground

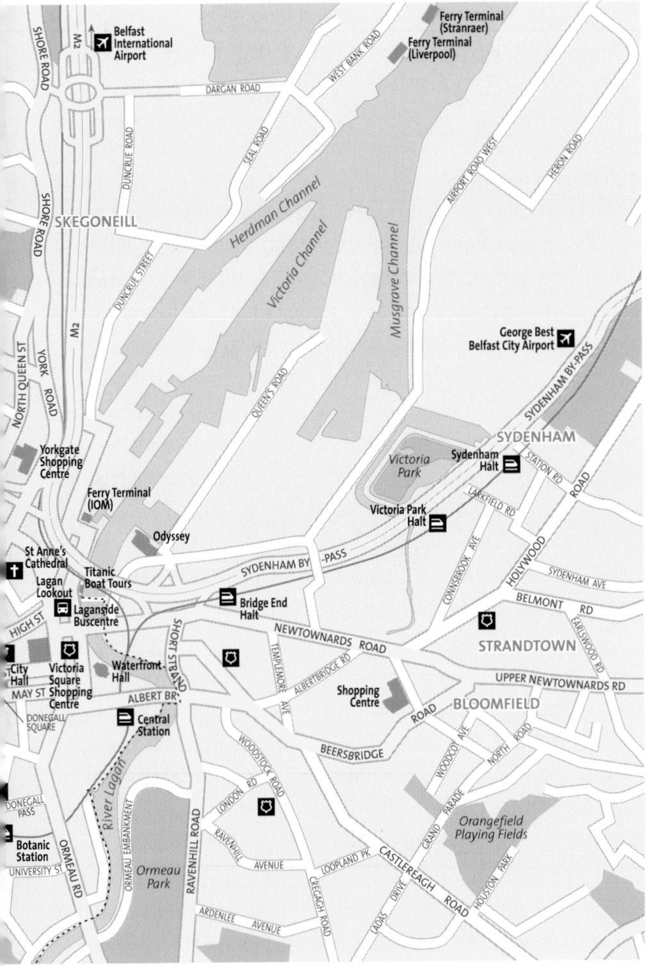

Belfast International Airport
Ferry Terminal (Stranraer)
Ferry Terminal (Liverpool)
SHORE ROAD
M2
DARGAN ROAD
WEST BANK ROAD
SEAL ROAD
DUNCRUE ROAD
AIRPORT ROAD WEST
HERON ROAD
SKEGONEILL
Herdman Channel
Victoria Channel
Musgrave Channel
DUNCRUE STREET
George Best Belfast City Airport
SYDENHAM BY-PASS
NORTH QUEEN ST
YORK ROAD
QUEEN'S ROAD
SYDENHAM
Yorkgate Shopping Centre
Victoria Park
Sydenham Halt
STATION RD
Ferry Terminal (IOM)
LARKFIELD RD
Victoria Park Halt
Odyssey
St Anne's Cathedral
SYDENHAM BY-PASS
CONNSBROOK AVE
HOLYWOOD ROAD
Titanic Boat Tours
Lagan Lookout
SYDENHAM AVE
Laganside Buscentre
Bridge End Halt
BELMONT RD
HIGH ST
SHORT STRAND
NEWTOWNARDS ROAD
EARLSWOOD RD
STRANDTOWN
TEMPLEMORE AVE
ALBERTBRIDGE RD
City Hall
Victoria Square Shopping Centre
Waterfront Hall
UPPER NEWTOWNARDS RD
MAY ST
ALBERT BR
Shopping Centre
BLOOMFIELD
DONEGALL SQUARE
Central Station
ROAD
WOODCOT AVE
NORTH ROAD
WOODSTOCK ROAD
BEERSBRIDGE
River Lagan
DONEGALL PASS
LONDON RD
GRAND PARADE
Orangefield Playing Fields
ORMEAU EMBANKMENT
RAVENHILL ROAD
RAVENHILL AVENUE
Botanic Station
ORMEAU RD
UNIVERSITY ST
Ormeau Park
LOOPLAND PK
CASTLEREAGH ROAD
HOUSTON PARK
CREAGH ROAD
LADAS DRIVE
ARDENLEE AVENUE

second floor with exhibits on both the history of the castle and Cave Hill Country Park (see page 80). ⓐ Antrim Road ⓣ 028 9077 6925 ⓦ www.belfastcastle.co.uk ◷ Visitor Centre 09.00–22.00 Mon–Sat, 09.00–18.00 Sun ⓝ Bus: 1A-D

Belfast City Cemetery

Belfast City Cemetery is a huge mixed cemetery located in a nationalist area. Before it opened in 1869, a wall was built underground to symbolically divide the Catholic and Protestant areas. Look out for the graves of some famous Belfast residents, including the writer Robert Wilson Lynd, Viscount Pirrie (chairman of Harland and Wolff during the building of the *Titanic*), Sir Edward Harland (one of the founders of Harland and Wolff) and Denis Donaldson, former IRA member and Sinn Féin official, who was killed in 2006 after it was announced that he had been a spy for the British Government. Tours are available. ⓐ Falls Road ⓣ 028 9032 0202 ◷ 08.00–18.00 Mon–Sat, 10.00–18.00 Sun (Mar & Oct); 08.00–18.00 Mon, Wed, Fri & Sat, 08.00–20.00 Tues & Thur, 10.00–18.00 Sun (Apr–Sept); 08.00–16.00 Mon–Sat, 10.00–16.00 Sun (Nov–Feb) ⓝ Bus: 10A-F

Belfast Zoo

Located in North Belfast near the Castle (see page 75), the zoo aims to help endangered animals from around the world. Visit zoo favourites such as the barbary lions, giraffes and elephants, but don't miss the red kangaroos and Malayan sun bears. The Bird Park has been renovated and here you'll see blue-bellied rollers and white-crested turacos, while the Rainforest House is home to Jasmine, the two-toed sloth. When it's sunny you can

sit and watch waterfowl and flamingos beside the lake while enjoying a picnic. Otherwise, you can tuck into hot food and drinks at the Ark Café. ⓐ Antrim Road ⓣ 028 9077 6277 ⓦ www.belfastzoo.co.uk ◷ 10.00–19.00 daily (Apr–Sept); 10.00–16.00 daily (Oct–Mar) (last admission two hours before closing) ⓝ Bus: 10A-F, 2A ⓘ Admission charge

Black Taxi Tours NI

A good alternative to other official tours, the Black Taxi Tours offer an insiders' view of the city. The tours take in the Shankill Road and Falls Road murals, Milltown Cemetery, Stormont, Queen's University, City Hall and Belfast Castle. It is more

Black Taxi Tours take in the famous murals

expensive, but you can stop to take pictures or buy souvenirs and can ask questions as you go. You can also hire cabs to go on a Causeway Coast tour or devise your own itinerary. ⓣ 028 9064 2264 ⓦ www.belfasttours.com ⓛ By arrangement ⓝ Drivers will pick you up at your hotel if required

Cave Hill Country Park

Rising up 368 m (1,207 ft) behind the city, Cave Hill is one of the city's most celebrated landmarks and the location of Belfast Castle (see page 75). Since 1992 it has been a Country Park and wildlife refuge for a variety of animals and birds, as well as containing two nature reserves, Ballyhagan and Hazelwood. One of the most noticeable features of the park is Napoleon's Nose, an outcrop on the top of the hill, which can be seen from the city centre. Also known as McArt's Fort, It was here that the leaders of the 1798 rebellion took an oath to fight for Ireland's liberation from English rule. You can discover more about the history of the area at the Visitor Centre inside the castle and also explore the park via waymarked paths. ⓐ Antrim Road ⓛ Dawn till dusk ⓝ Bus: 1A-F

Coiste Political Tours

Another way to see the city is to take a tour round republican areas with the ex-prisoner community. Starting from Divis Tower at the Westlink end of the Falls Road, you get to hear some very different viewpoints on the conflict. The walking tours last around two hours, but booking is essential – you can even organise tours in Spanish, Basque, Irish or French. ⓐ Divis Tower, Falls Road ⓣ 028 9020 0770 ⓦ www.coiste.ie ⓛ Walking tour:

11.00 Mon–Sat, 14.00 Sun Walk or take a collective black taxi from Castle Street car park Admission charge

Crumlin Road Gaol

This former prison was opened in the 19th century and finally closed in 1996. It held political prisoners throughout the 20th century and became notorious during the Troubles as a remand centre. The jail is currently undergoing major refurbishment to make it more accessible for visits. Until it is completed in 2011, tours of the jail are suspended. Crumlin Road 028 9024 6609 Call for updated opening hours Bus: 12

Divis Tower

Divis Tower might seem like any ordinary tower block, but from the 1970s the top two floors were occupied by the British Army as a lookout point over Divis flats around the tower (which were demolished in the early 1980s), up the Falls Road and towards the city centre. The troops finally moved out in 2005, but the tower is still an iconic building in the history of the Troubles. Divis Street Walk from city centre or take a black taxi from Castle Street car park

Garden of Remembrance

Walking up the Falls Road, just before you arrive at the library and Sinn Féin bookshop on the right-hand side, you'll see a small garden on the left. This is one of many memorials to those who died in the Troubles. Being in the Falls Road, this is dedicated to republicans (including the hunger striker Bobby Sands), with the

Irish tricolour flying above. ⓐ Falls Road ⓝ Walk from city centre or take a black taxi from Castle Street car park

Milltown Cemetery

Located along the Falls Road, this is a Catholic cemetery where you'll find IRA and other republican memorials. A sea of Celtic crosses, the cemetery has a backdrop of the Belfast hills and views across the M1 motorway towards the city centre. Look out for the green field of unmarked paupers' graves, where victims of cholera, typhoid and flu were buried. ⓐ Falls Road ⓝ Bus: 10A-F. Walk from city centre or take a black taxi from Castle Street car park

Orange Hall

As you cross the Westlink towards Crumlin Road, you will see an Orange Hall on the left-hand side. On the top is a statue of 'King Billy', William of Orange, who defeated King James I in the

MILLTOWN: REFLECTING BELFAST'S TROUBLED PAST

In 1988 the loyalist paramilitary Michael Stone killed two mourners and a Provisional IRA member, and injured around 50 more people at a funeral at Milltown Cemetery for the Gibraltar Three (three IRA members killed by the SAS in Gibraltar). The cemetery also contains the graves of Bobby Sands and the other hunger strikers who died in 1981. Look at the plots more carefully and you'll notice that the republican plots are divided up into Official IRA, Provisional IRA, INLA and Real IRA.

A sea of Celtic crosses: Milltown Cemetery

famous Battle of the Boyne in 1690. Today, the hall is a renowned starting point for Orange Order marches. ⓐ Carlisle Circus Ⓝ Bus: 1A, 1B, 1E

Peace Line

This is a steel wall that divides the nationalist Falls Road area from the loyalist Shankill Road. The best way to see it is on the Belfast bus tour. ⓐ West Belfast Ⓝ Bus: 10A-F

St Peter's Cathedral

Belfast's Roman Catholic cathedral was built in the 19th century to cope with the large numbers of workers who had come to work in the linen mills nearby. Its position made it a prominent landmark with five doorways, two porch entrances and a sculpture depicting the liberation of St Peter from prison over the main entrance, plus its iconic twin spires, which were added a few years later. ⓐ St Peter's Square, off Albert Street ⓣ 028 9032 7573 ⓕ 028 9032 5570 ⓦ www.stpeterscathedralbelfast.com ⓛ Mass: 10.00 Mon–Sat, 19.30 Tues & Thur, 09.00, 11.00 & 19.00 Sun

West Belfast murals

The political murals in West Belfast have become one of the city's most popular tourist attractions. You can get a quick overview on a bus tour, but to get a closer look you either need to take a private Black Taxi Tour (see pages 79–80) or go on foot. There are some interesting murals in East Belfast too, but they are not as accessible as those along the nationalist Falls Road and the loyalist Shankill Road. You'll see murals on the side of virtually every corner building along the streets. In the Falls Road these range from murals showing sympathy for other nationalist and liberation movements, such as those in Palestine and Catalonia, and images depicting the 1916 Easter Rising, hunger strikers and other 'fallen' IRA comrades. Along the Shankill Road you can see images of the Derry Apprentice Boys slamming the gates of the city in 1688 and the Battle of the Boyne in 1690, as well as murals supporting loyalist paramilitary groups such as the Ulster Volunteer Force (UVF) and Ulster Defence Association (UDA). ⓐ Falls and Shankill roads Ⓝ Sightseeing bus tour, Black Taxi Tour or on foot

CULTURE

Cultúrlann McAdam

The centre of the Falls Road Gaeltacht (Irish-speaking) community, Cultúrlann McAdam runs Irish language courses, has a bookshop and tourist point (with help on accommodation), and hosts art, music, drama and literature events. Hear some live traditional Irish music in the café/restaurant every week – they welcome passing musicians too! Buy an Irish language course in the shop, hear locals chatting in Irish in the café or stay for one of the other cultural events. ⓐ 216 Falls Road ⓣ 028 9096 4180 ⓦ www.culturlann.com Ⓛ 09.00–21.00 Mon–Fri, 09.00–18.00 Sat & Sun Ⓝ Any bus from Queen Street in the city centre

RETAIL THERAPY

At Cultúrlann there's a selection of Irish language and literature books as well as cards and photographs. In Andersonstown there's a large O'Neills International Sportswear shop selling the Gaelic football strip, hurley sticks and balls, Ireland rugby tops and Celtic football tops.

TAKING A BREAK

The Ark Café £ ❶ Located in Belfast Zoo, this is a good option for the family with hot and cold food and veggie options.
ⓐ Belfast Zoo ⓣ 028 9077 6925 ⓦ www.belfastzoo.co.uk
◷ 10.30–17.30 daily (Apr–Sept); 10.30–15.30 daily (Oct–Mar)

Cultúrlann Café Bistro £ ❷ You can stop here for a late lunch, afternoon refreshments or dinner at a reasonable price, while listening to locals chatting in Irish (see page 85). The menu includes fish and chips, lasagne, burgers, wraps and pizza.
ⓐ 216 Falls Road ⓣ 028 9096 4180 ⓦ www.culturlann.com
◷ 09.00–21.00 Mon–Fri, 09.00–18.00 Sat & Sun

Northern Culture £ ❸ Located on the Shankill Road, this modern café promotes Northern Irish culture – its poets, Ulster-Scots language and music. It's a good place to stop for soup and a sarnie, and you can also book city and coastal tours from here.
ⓐ 195 Shankill Road ⓣ 028 9033 2806 ◷ 10.00–20.00 Mon–Fri, 10.00–19.00 Sat, closed Sun

AFTER DARK

RESTAURANTS

Sopranos £ ❹ This favourite North Belfast restaurant serves a vast range of food options all day, from Ulster fries for breakfast to ribs and Soprano's classic 12-inch pizzas at lunch and dinner. ⓐ 529 Antrim Road ⓣ 028 9077 1062 ⓦ www.sopranosbelfast.com ⓛ 09.00–22.00 daily

Cellar Restaurant ££ ❺ This is Belfast Castle's restaurant and serves quality home-grown food in a beautiful historic location. ⓐ Belfast Castle, off Antrim Road ⓣ 028 9077 6925 ⓦ www.belfastcastle.co.uk ⓛ 11.00–17.00 daily (snacks/light refreshments), 12.30–15.00 (lunch) Mon–Sat, 12.30–16.00 Sun, 17.00–18.30 (early evening meal), 19.00–21.00 (dinner) Tues–Sat

PUBS

The Beehive A lively local pub with pub grub from fish and chips to curry, plus folk sessions on a Sunday. ⓐ 193 Falls Road ⓣ 028 9032 8439 ⓛ 11.30–23.00 Mon–Sat, 12.00–22.30 Sun

McEnaney's Located opposite Milltown Cemetery, this traditional pub is great for a pint or two after a long walk from the city centre. If you're lucky you might hear some live traditional music. ⓐ Glen Road, Andersonstown ⓣ 028 9061 3951 ⓛ 11.30–24.00 Mon–Sat, 12.00–24.00 Sun

The Whitefort Pub Traditional Victorian pub with original décor and tiled floor, this is what was considered a 'man's pub', where men would bring their wives at weekends only. Women are now welcome any night of the week (who said Emily Davison died in vain?), and no longer have to drink separately upstairs! ⓐ Lower Springfield Road ⓛ 11.30–23.00 Mon–Sat, 12.00–22.30 Sun

South & East Belfast

South and East Belfast are adjacent but contrasting areas of Belfast. As the location of Queen's University, the South is considered to be the intellectual centre, but its large student population also gives it a bohemian feel. Cheap student terraced accommodation backs on to leafy avenues of expensive houses; boutique hotels and designer clothes shops along the Lisburn Road lead into wild nights in Bradbury Place and Botanic Avenue. You can walk to Botanic easily from the city centre and even down to Queen's University if you have the feet for it. Beyond that and you'll have to think about taking a bus. Make time to see East Belfast, primarily a residential area but also the location of some key attractions and the gateway to North Down. Take a tour around the Titanic Quarter, the target of a huge makeover that will transform the area and bring work, play, arts, cafés and hotels.

SIGHTS & ATTRACTIONS

Belfast Walking Tour

In the lead-up to RMS *Titanic*'s centenary commemorations in 2012, this gentle tour is a good introduction to the main places associated with the ship. The two-hour walk visits SS *Nomadic*, the White Star Line ship that transported first-class passengers to the ship, as well as the former offices of famous shipbuilders Harland and Wolff, the ship's slipway, Titanic Dock and the Pump House and café. ⓐ Starts at the Odyssey complex ⓣ 07904 350 339 ⓦ www.titanicwalk.com ⓛ 11.00 & 14.00 daily ❶ Booking advised

Botanic Gardens Park

Highlights of the park are the restored Victorian Palm House, with a valuable collection of tropical and temperate palms, and Tropical Ravine, with a humid jungle glen and a fish pond filled with giant water lilies. Today, it is popular with both locals and visitors for walking, relaxing and taking in the sights and sounds, including occasional music events, from pop and classical concerts to the Belfast Taste and Music Fest in August. ⓐ Stranmillis Road/Botanic Avenue ⓣ 028 9032 0202 Ⓛ Dawn till dusk Ⓝ Bus: 8 to Queens University or 7 to College Park

Lagan Valley Regional Park

This park was established in 1967 and extends more than 16 km (10 miles) from Stranmillis in South Belfast to Lisburn's Union

The Palm House at the Botanic Gardens

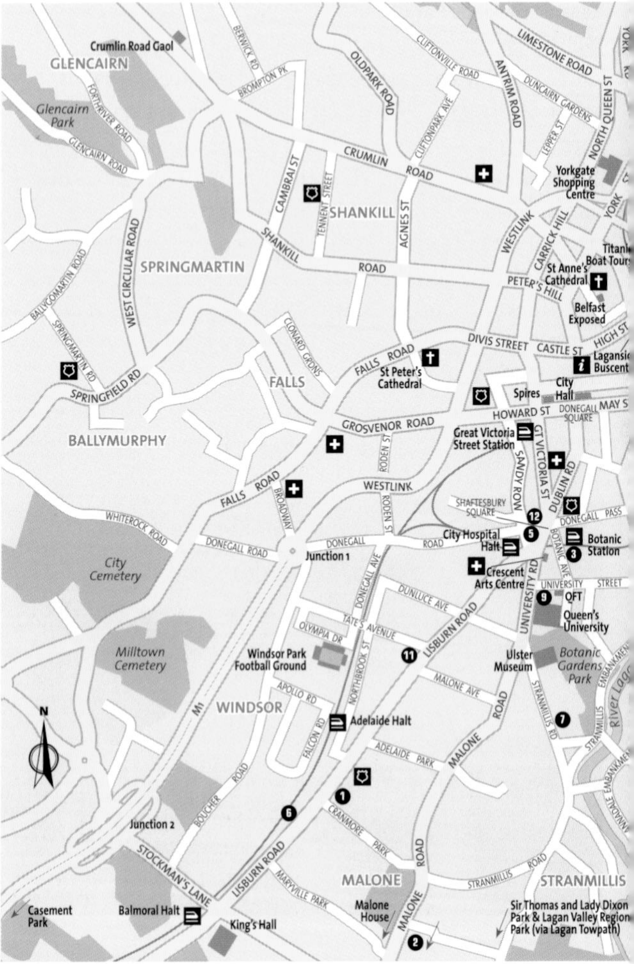

Crumlin Road Gaol
GLENCAIRN
Glencairn Park
FORTHRIVER ROAD
GLENCAIRN ROAD
BERWICK RD
BROMPTON PK
OLDPARK ROAD
CLIFTONVILLE ROAD
CLIFTONPARK AVE
ANTRIM ROAD
LIMESTONE ROAD
DUNCAIRN GARDENS
LEPPER ST
NORTH QUEEN ST
YORK
CRUMLIN ROAD
CAMBRAI ST
TENNENT STREET
SHANKILL
AGNES ST
WESTLINK
Yorkgate Shopping Centre
CARRICK HILL
YORK
Titanic Boat Tours
St Anne's Cathedral
PETER'S HILL
Belfast Exposed
BALLYGOMARTIN ROAD
WEST CIRCULAR ROAD
SPRINGMARTIN
SHANKILL ROAD
SPRINGMARTIN RD
CLONARD GDNS
DIVIS STREET
CASTLE ST
HIGH ST
SPRINGFIELD RD
FALLS ROAD
St Peter's Cathedral
Lagan Buscent
FALLS
Spires
City Hall
HOWARD ST
DONEGALL SQUARE
MAY ST
GROSVENOR ROAD
Great Victoria Street Station
BALLYMURPHY
RODEN ST
GT VICTORIA ST
SANDY ROW
DUBLIN RD
FALLS ROAD
BROADWAY
WESTLINK
SHAFTESBURY SQUARE
WHITEROCK ROAD
RODEN ST
12
DONEGALL PASS
5
City Hospital Halt
Botanic Station
DONEGALL ROAD
DONEGALL ROAD
Junction 1
BOTANIC AVE
3
City Cemetery
DONEGALL AVE
Crescent Arts Centre
UNIVERSITY RD
UNIVERSITY STREET
DUNLUCE AVE
9
QFT
TATE'S AVENUE
LISBURN ROAD
Queen's University
OLYMPIA DR
Milltown Cemetery
Windsor Park Football Ground
NORTHBROOK ST
11
Ulster Museum
Botanic Gardens Park
EMBANKMENT
MALONE AVE
APOLLO RD
M1
WINDSOR
Adelaide Halt
MALONE ROAD
STRANMILLIS RD
7
STRANMILLIS
River Lagan
N
FALCON RD
ADELAIDE PARK
BOUCHER ROAD
1
ANNADALE EMBANKMENT
6
CRANMORE PARK
Junction 2
STOCKMAN'S LANE
LISBURN ROAD
ROAD
MALONE
STRANMILLIS ROAD
STRANMILLIS
MARYVILLE PARK
Malone House
MALONE
Casement Park
Balmoral Halt
King's Hall
2
Sir Thomas and Lady Dixon Park & Lagan Valley Regional Park (via Lagan Towpath)

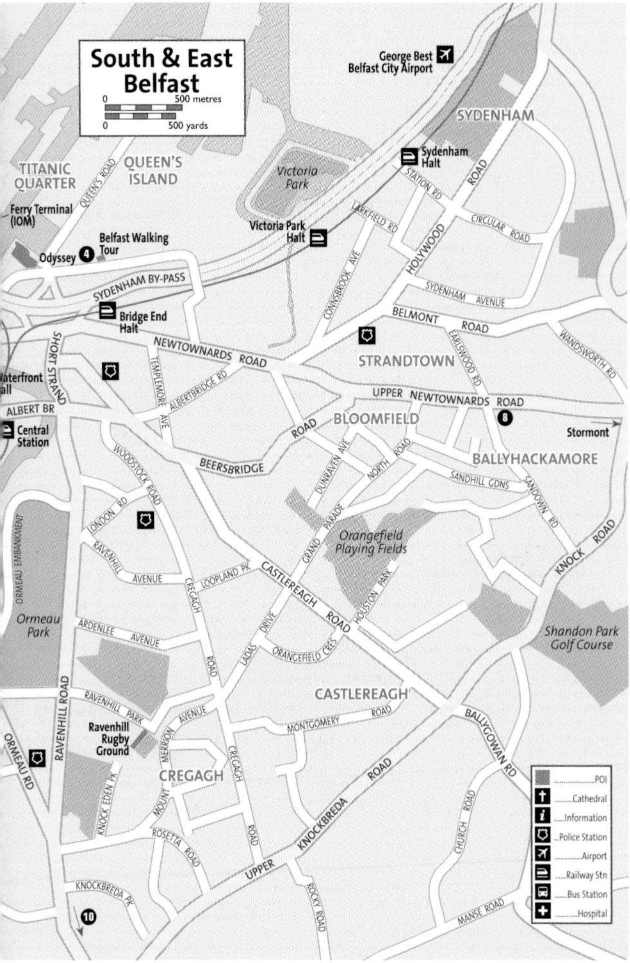

South & East Belfast

0 500 metres
0 500 yards

George Best Belfast City Airport
SYDENHAM
Sydenham Halt
TITANIC QUARTER
QUEEN'S ISLAND
QUEEN'S ROAD
Victoria Park
Ferry Terminal (IOM)
Victoria Park Halt
Belfast Walking Tour
Odyssey 4
STATION RD
LARKFIELD RD
CIRCULAR ROAD
HOLYWOOD ROAD
SYDENHAM BY-PASS
CONNSBROOK AVE
SYDENHAM AVENUE
Bridge End Halt
BELMONT ROAD
SHORT STRAND
NEWTOWNARDS ROAD
STRANDTOWN
EARLSWOOD RD
WANDSWORTH RD
Waterfront Hall
TEMPLEMORE AVE
ALBERTBRIDGE RD
UPPER NEWTOWNARDS ROAD
ALBERT BR
Central Station
BLOOMFIELD
8
Stormont
ROAD
BEERSBRIDGE
WOODSTOCK ROAD
DUNRAVEN AVE
NORTH ROAD
BALLYHACKAMORE
SANDHILL GDNS
SANDOWN RD
LONDON RD
GRAND PARADE
Orangefield Playing Fields
KNOCK ROAD
ORMEAU EMBANKMENT
RAVENHILL AVENUE
LOOPLAND PK
CASTLEREAGH ROAD
HOUSTON PARK
CREGAGH ROAD
Ormeau Park
ARDENLEE AVENUE
LADAS DRIVE
ORANGEFIELD CRES
Shandon Park Golf Course
CASTLEREAGH
RAVENHILL ROAD
RAVENHILL PARK
AVENUE
MONTGOMERY ROAD
BALLYGOWAN RD
Ravenhill Rugby Ground
MERRION
ORMEAU RD
CREGAGH
CREGAGH ROAD
MOUNT
KNOCK EDEN PK
KNOCKBREDA ROAD
CHURCH ROAD
ROSETTA ROAD
UPPER
ROCKY ROAD
KNOCKBREDA PK
10
MANSE ROAD

POI
Cathedral
Information
Police Station
Airport
Railway Stn
Bus Station
Hospital

Locks. The reach of the park means it is a mosaic of countryside, urban parks, heritage sites, nature reserves and the Lagan Towpath. ⓐ Lockview Road to Lisburn Union Locks ⓣ 028 9049 1922 ⓦ www.laganvalley.co.uk ⓛ 24 hours ⓝ Bus: 8A-C

Malone House

Malone House is an elegant late Georgian manor located in the South Belfast parkland known as the Barnett Demesne, itself part of the Lagan Valley Regional Park. You can walk through woodland, meadows and marsh. Look out for rabbits, foxes, mink, otters, bats and long-eared owls. ⓐ Barnett Demesne, Malone Road ⓣ 028 9068 1246 ⓦ www.malonehouse.co.uk ⓛ Park: 24 hours, Malone House: 09.00–17.00 Mon–Sat, 12.00–17.00 Sun ⓝ Bus: 9A-C

Odyssey

A Landmark Millennium Project for Northern Ireland, the Odyssey complex is divided into three main parts:

W5 (ⓦ www.w5online.co.uk) is an interactive discovery centre with four dynamic exhibition areas, Start, Go, See and Do, with changing temporary exhibitions. Here, children (and adults) make a voyage of discovery. You can find out what it's like to be a car mechanic, explore your senses with the sounds and feel of nature in a woodland area, beat the lie detector and bring robots to life.

Odyssey Arena (ⓦ www.odysseyarena.com) is home to the Belfast Giants ice hockey team and also hosts touring shows, exhibitions and concerts.

Odyssey Pavilion (ⓦ www.odysseypavilion.com) is where you'll find an IMAX cinema, ten-pin bowling, bars, restaurants and a nightclub, plus a large car park. ⓐ Queen's Quay ⓣ 028 9045 8806

Various Bus: Laganside or shuttle bus during major events from various city-centre pick-up points Admission charge

Ormeau Park

Once part of the demesne of the Donegall family, the estate was sold to the Belfast Corporation in the late 19th century, becoming the first public park in Belfast. It remains one of the largest in the city with woodland, wildlife and nature trails, and hosts various events throughout the year. Ormeau Road 028 9049 1813 Dawn till dusk Bus: 7A, 7D

Queen's University

Founded by Queen Victoria, Queen's University opened in 1840 in the magnificent Lanyon Building, still the most recognisable part of the university. Since then, the university estate has grown to include more than 300 buildings. There is a visitor centre inside the Lanyon Building, with a gift shop and exhibitions. University Road 028 9097 5252

Queen's University, built in prosperous Victorian times

ⓦ www.qub.ac.uk ⓛ Welcome Centre: 10.00–16.30 Mon–Sat, 10.00–13.00 Sun (May–Sept Sat & Sun only) ⓑ Bus: 8A-C

Stormont

The home of the Northern Ireland Assembly, this neoclassical building is located at the end of Prince of Wales Avenue. George Best's funeral was held here in 2005. Unfortunately, visitors can't go inside, but they can walk along the avenue and in the grounds. ⓐ Upper Newtownards Road ⓦ www.niassembly.gov.uk ⓑ Bus: 23 to Stormont Massey Avenue Gates

Titanic Boat Tours

This water tour is a great way to learn all about the *Titanic*. You'll see the offices where the ship was designed, the dry dock where it was worked on and the slipways where it first took to water. ⓐ No 2 jetty, Donegall Quay ⓣ 028 9033 0844 or 07718 910 423 ⓦ www.laganboatcompany.com ⓛ 12.30, 14.00 & 15.30 daily (Apr–Sept); 12.30, 14.00 & 15.30 Sat & Sun (Oct–Dec); 12.30 & 14.00 Sat & Sun (Jan–Mar) ⓑ Bus: Laganside Buscentre ⓘ Book in advance. Admission charge

Titanic Quarter

Once the centre of Belfast's great shipbuilding industry, today the former shipyards on Queen's Island are referred to as the Titanic Quarter, as the RMS *Titanic* was designed and built here by the shipbuilding firm Harland and Wolff, which was set up in the 1860s. Today, the company is a leader in ship repair, design and structural engineering, and the shipyards are once again seeing some activity with new plans for development. Harland

Samson and Goliath: landmarks in their own right

BUILDING THE *TITANIC*

By the time Edward Harland died in 1895, Harland and Wolff had become the world's greatest shipbuilders. Designed by Alexander Carlisle and then Thomas Andrews, the floating palace that was the *Titanic* was launched on 31 May 1911 in front of thousands of onlookers. It was taken to Southampton and set off on its maiden voyage from there on 10 April 1912. Four days later, having travelled 2,400 km (1,500 miles), the ship struck an iceberg and was fatally damaged. Of the 2,228 passengers and crew, only 705 survived.

and Wolff's two yellow cranes, known as Samson and Goliath, stand as a monument to the great shipbuilding era, but around them a new era has begun. As part of the development over the next decade, apartments, hotels, offices, marinas and cultural spaces are already being built onsite. Visitors can visit the drawing offices, dock and pump house where RMS *Titanic* had its final fit-out. Take the Belfast Citysightseeing tour bus (see page 58) and hop off here to visit the Dry Dock and pump room and HMS *Caroline*. ⓐ Queen's Island ⓦ www.titanicquarter.com
Ⓣ Bus: Laganside Buscentre or Belfast Citysightseeing tour bus

CULTURE

Belfast Exposed

This contemporary photography gallery provides a great insight into the life of Belfast and its residents both past and present.

As well as temporary exhibitions, it runs photography and image-making courses, and has a darkroom and Mac digital suite for hire. ⓐ The Exchange Place, 23 Donegall Street ⓣ 028 9023 0965 ⓛ By appointment

Crescent Arts Centre

Housed in a former girls' school, this arts centre hosts workshops, education/outreach classes, exhibitions and events from drama, dance and movement to music. ⓐ 2–4 University Road ⓣ 028 9024 2338 ⓦ www.crescentarts. org ⓛ 10.00–22.00 variable Mon–Fri, 10.00–19.00 variable Sat Ⓣ Bus: 9A-C ⓘ Admission charge

King's Hall

This large venue hosts exhibitions, conferences and events from home, dog and bike shows to concerts and boxing matches. ⓐ Lisburn Road, Balmoral ⓣ 028 9066 5225 ⓦ www.kingshall.co.uk ⓛ Performance times vary – check website for details Ⓣ Train: Balmoral Halt; Bus: 9B/9A to Lisburn Road ⓘ Admission charge

The Naughton Gallery at Queen's

Located inside Queen's University, this gallery exhibits works from the university's own collection as well as touring exhibitions and shows by local and international artists. It's only been in business since 2001, but its dynamism and verve have already won it a reputation as one of the leading academic-institution *vitrines* in Europe; and quite right, too – no stuffy, conservative gallery, this, the Naughton encourages

experimental artists and fosters the development of promising newcomers. It also regularly stages fascinating lectures by visiting glitter-arty types. ⓐ Lanyon Building, Queen's University ⓣ 028 9097 3580 ⓦ www.naughtongallery.org ⓛ 11.00–16.00 Mon–Sat, closed Sun ⓡ Bus: 8A-C

Queen's Film Theatre (QFT)
Ireland's longest-established cultural cinema, the QFT, screens both classics and contemporary films. ⓐ 20 University Square ⓣ 028 9097 1097 ⓦ www.queensfilmtheatre.com ⓛ Screening times vary – check website for details ⓡ Bus: 8A-C ⓘ Admission charge

Ulster Museum
Relaunched in 2009 after a three-year redevelopment, the Ulster Museum has a much larger space to spread its wide-ranging collections of art, archaeology and history. You'll need a few hours to get the most of the museum, so you're better off picking a few favourite areas. Some of the highlights include jewellery and armour from medieval Ireland, as well as displays dedicated to the Troubles, the Armada, Peter the Polar Bear and Patrick the champion Irish wolfhound. There are also collections of British masterpiece paintings by the likes of Thomas Gainsborough and Sir Joshua Reynolds, European and Asian decorative art, a huge array of animals and plant life, and fossils and minerals. ⓐ Botanic Gardens, Stranmillis Road ⓣ 028 9038 3000 ⓦ www.ulstermuseum.org.uk ⓛ 10.00–17.00 Tues–Sun, closed Mon (except on bank holidays) ⓡ Train: Botanic; Bus: 8A/8B from Donegall Square East

TAKING A BREAK

Clements £ ❶ One of a small chain of coffee bars with three outlets in Belfast. They pride themselves on their quality coffee and cakes. ⓐ 342 Lisburn Road ⓣ 028 9033 1827 ⓛ 08.00–24.00 Mon–Thur, 08.00–23.00 Fri, 09.00–23.00 Sat, 10.00–23.00 Sun

Lock Keeper's Inn £ ❷ Made famous by a scandal involving the First Minister's wife, this café-restaurant has maintained its composure. It's a good stop-off if you're walking along the Lagan Towpath. You can have French toast for breakfast, paninis and pitta pockets for lunch, as well as hot options from spaghetti carbonara to stuffed peppers. ⓐ 2 Lock Keeper's Lane ⓣ 028 9069 3953 ⓛ 08.30–17.00 Tues–Fri, 08.00–18.00 Sat & Sun, closed Mon

Maggie May's Belfast Café £ ❸ This is the place to come for hangover food or if you're just after a good Ulster fry for breakfast. ⓐ 50 Botanic Avenue ⓣ 028 9032 2662 ⓛ 08.00–22.30 Mon–Sat, 10.00–22.30 Sun

Pump House Café £ ❹ This café at the *Titanic*'s Dock and Pump House is a convenient place to stop for a light sandwich and soup lunch or just for a quick coffee and a bun. ⓐ NI Science Park, Queen's Road, Queen's Island ⓣ 028 9073 7813 ⓛ 10.30–16.00 daily

Revelations Internet Café £ ❺ Grab a frappucino, ice-cream milkshake or herbal tea and check your email at the same time.

ⓐ 27 Shaftesbury Square ⓣ 028 9032 0337 ⓦ www.revelations.co.uk ◷ 08.00–22.00 Mon–Fri, 10.00–18.00 Sat, 11.00–19.00 Sun

Springsteen's Diner £–££ ❻ A lively American-style diner where you can tuck into chunky homemade burgers, steaks and fajitas, washed down with a pitcher of beer. ⓐ 633 Lisburn Road ⓣ 028 9066 7272 ◷ 10.00–22.00 Mon–Fri, 09.00–22.00 Sat & Sun

AFTER DARK

RESTAURANTS

The Blue Print Pizza Company £ ❼ Easy lunch or dinner stop in the heart of the university district with pizzas, pasta and salads. ⓐ 92 Stranmillis Road ⓣ 028 9066 3101 ⓦ www.blueprintpizza.com ◷ 11.00–23.00 Mon–Sat, 13.00–23.00 Sun

Alden's Restaurant ££ ❽ Modern restaurant with a varied menu that attracts local celebrities and politicians. ⓐ 229 Upper Newtownards Road ⓣ 028 9065 0079 ⓦ www.aldensrestaurant.com ◷ 10.00–22.00 Mon–Thur, 10.00–23.00 Fri & Sat, 12.00–16.30 Sun

Beatrice Kennedy ££ ❾ One of Belfast's finest restaurants, there's an intimate but relaxed atmosphere here and a modern menu that features the likes of hot smoked salmon with beetroot confit, seared local scallops and Barbary duck with polenta mash. ⓐ 44 University Road ⓣ 028 9020 2290 ⓦ www.beatricekennedy.co.uk ◷ 17.00–22.15 Tues–Sat, 12.30–14.30 & 17.00–20.15 Sun, closed Mon

Four Winds ££ ⓾ Venue divided into three parts: the top-floor Ink Restaurant with panoramic city views; slick Four Winds Wine Bar; and Lounge, a relaxing space to watch football and rugby matches. ⓐ 111 Newton Park ⓣ 028 9070 7970 ⓦ www.thefourwinds.co.uk ⓛ Variable

Shu Restaurant ££ ⓫ Brasserie-style ground-floor restaurant, basement cocktail and tapas bar with top Belfast DJs on the decks every Wednesday. ⓐ 253 Lisburn Road ⓣ 028 9038 1655 ⓦ www.shu-restaurant.com ⓛ 12.00–14.30 & 18.00–22.00 Mon–Sat, closed Sun

Cayenne £££ ⓬ Award-winning restaurant owned by celebrity chefs Paul and Jeanne Rankin, serving modern Irish cuisine with an international flavour. ⓐ 7 Ascot House, Shaftesbury Square ⓣ 028 9033 1532 ⓦ www.cayenne-restaurant.co.uk ⓛ 12.00–14.15 Thur & Fri, 12.00–16.00 Sun, 17.00–23.00 daily

PUBS & CLUBS

The Botanic Inn Another favourite pub with three different bars offering live sports, pub grub, live music and the odd pub quiz. ⓐ 23–27 Malone Road ⓣ 028 9050 9740 ⓦ www.thebotanicinn.com ⓛ 11.30–01.00 Mon–Sat, 12.00–24.00 Sun

Empire Music Hall Legendary establishment with a basement pub-style bar and old theatre-style upper venue with a stage featuring salsa classes, live music and comedy. ⓐ 42 Botanic

Avenue ⓣ 028 9024 9276 ⓦ www.thebelfastempire.com ◷ 11.00–01.00 Mon–Sat, 11.00–24.00 Sun

The King's Head This renovated Lisburn pub now has a restaurant and a beer garden. Grab a gastro-sandwich or wrap for lunch, or tuck into dinners of rare-breed bangers and mash or Northern Irish chargrilled steaks. ⓐ 829 Lisburn Road ⓣ 028 9050 9950 ⓦ www.kingsheadbelfast.com ◷ 12.00–24.00 Sun & Mon, 12.00–01.00 Tues–Sat, restaurant 12.00–21.00 Sun, 18.30–21.30 Tues–Sat

Lavery's Bar and Gin Palace Golden Mile venue notorious for the interesting characters who hang out here. A good raucous night out with food, music, pool hall, DJs and live music. ⓐ Bradbury Place, off Shaftesbury Square ⓣ 028 9087 1106 ⓦ www.laverysbelfast.com ◷ 12.00–late

Madison's Boutique hotel with a café-bar upstairs serving food, beer and cocktails all day, with live music and club nights on Mondays and Fridays in The Avenue downstairs. ⓐ 59–63 Botanic Avenue ⓣ 028 9050 9800 ⓦ www.madisonshotel.com ◷ 07.00–01.00 (food until 21.00 Sun–Thur, 22.00 Fri & Sat)

The Ulster Folk and Transport Museum: a glimpse of Northern Irish traditions, past and present

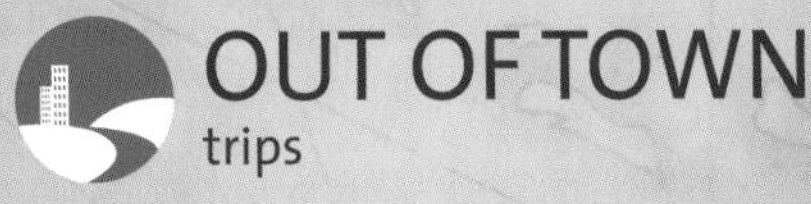

OUT OF TOWN
trips

Bangor & County Down

County Down is within easy reach of Belfast city centre. A few kilometres past George Best City Airport and the horizon widens as you head towards Holywood and Bangor overlooking Belfast Lough, an easy reach for day trips to the beach, country parks and the award-winning Ulster Folk & Transport Museum. South of here is Strangford Lough, with the Ards Peninsula on its east side. A trip to Downpatrick, one of the most important Christian sites in the country and the resting place of Ireland's patron saint, St Patrick, is also possible in a day. With a few extra days you could spend some time in the seaside resort of Newcastle, tasting some of the freshest seafood, climbing the peaks of the Mourne Mountains and exploring the Norman castle at Dundrum.

GETTING THERE

There are various routes out of Belfast to County Down by car. For North Down, head out on the A2 past George Best City Airport to Holywood and Bangor or take the A20 to Newtownards, which continues along the eastern banks of Strangford Lough to Portaferry. Alternatively, you can take the A21/A22 down the west side towards Downpatrick. For Dundrum, Newcastle and the Mourne Mountains go south out of the city along the A24, and for Hillsborough take the M1 and A1.

Trains leave Central Station to Holywood and Bangor. Buses for Newtownards and Portaferry leave from Laganside Buscentre, but for Hillsborough, Downpatrick and Newcastle, you'll need to go to Europa Buscentre.

SIGHTS & ATTRACTIONS

Ballyholme Beach

Ballyholme is a small coastal village between Bangor and Groomsport (see pages 108–9), best known for its 1.6 km- (1 mile-) long sandy beach. It's a favourite with families due to its gentle surf and the nearby nature reserve at Ballymacormick Point. ⓐ Ballyholme ⓦ Bus: BE4 (from Bangor)

Bangor

Bangor is a large seaside town with plenty of hotels, restaurants and entertainment, and is popular with tourists during the summer months. **Bangor Marina** is one of the largest in Northern Ireland. Look out for the rare colony of guillemots nesting in the harbour wall – they're also known as 'Bangor penguins'. Other highlights include: **Bangor Abbey**, a mixture of 15th–19th-century architecture; **Bangor Castle**, an Elizabethan-Jacobean-style mansion that is now actually the town hall; and the **Tower House** on Bangor seafront, which was built in 1637 as the Custom House and today is home to the tourist information centre. ⓐ Bangor, Down ⓣ Bangor Tourist Information 028 9127 0069 ⓦ Train: Bangor

Downpatrick

The county town of County Down, Downpatrick is associated with St Patrick, who is buried in the cemetery of **Down Cathedral**, along with St Columba and St Bridget. St Patrick is said to have brought Christianity to Ireland and for this reason this site is considered one of the holiest Christian sites in Ireland, dating from way before the construction of the

Culdaff
Clonmany
Portrush
Inishowen Head
Carrickart
Portstewart
2198
Muckish Mountain
Creeslough
Lough Swilly
Carrowkeel
Lough Foyle
City of Derry
Coleraine
N56
A2
A37
N13
DERRY
Limavady
Letterkenny
Derryveagh Mountains
St Johnstown
N14
Foyle
A5
A6
Claudy
Killygordon
N15
Strabane
Blue Stack Mountains
Draperstown
NORTHERN IRELAND
Newtownstewart
Derg
Donegal
A505
Creggan
Cookstown
A29
Omagh
Clonelly
A32
A47
Lower Lough Erne
A35
Dungannon
A46
Irvinestown
A4
Blaney
Aughnacloy
Enniskillen
Armagh
A28
A3
N16
Termon
Upper Lough Erne
Lisnaskea
A34
Monaghan
N12
Keady
A509
Clones
N87
Finn
Ballybay
N2
Castleblaney
REPUBLIC OF IRELAND
N3
N54

Belfast region

0 20 km
0 10 miles

ushmills & Bushmills Distillery
Whitepark Bay
Rathlin Island
Carrick-a-Rede Rope Bridge
Ballycastle Bay
Ballintoy
Ballycastle
Giant's Causeway
unluce astle
Armoy
Cushendun
Ballymoney
Antrim Hills
Cushendall
Glenariff Forest Park
Carnlough
Clogh
Glens of Antrim
Glenarm
The Maidens
(Antrim Coast Road)
Ballygally Head
M2
Larne
allymena
Moorfields
Portmuck
The Gobbins
M22
Ballyclare
M2
Carrickfergus
Carrickfergus Castle
Antrim
Belfast International
Holywood
Bangor
Ballyholme Beach
Newtownabbey
Groomsport
Lough Neagh
George Best Belfast City
Ulster Folk and Transport Museum
BELFAST
Scrabo Hill Country Park
Newtownards
Lisburn
Ards Peninsula
Comber
M1
Sprucefield
Strangford Lough
Lurgan
Hillsborough
Portadown
Portavogie
Castle Ward
Portaferry
Bann
Banbridge
Inch Abbey
Exploris
Downpatrick
Poyntz Pass
Castlewellan
Dundrum
Dundrum Castle
Ardglass
Tollymore Forest Park
852 Slieve Donard
Newcastle
Newry
Dundrum Bay
Mourne Mountains
Glasdrumman
Rostrevor
SCOTLAND
Stranraer

City
Large Town
Small Town
POI
Motorway
Main Road
Minor Road
Airport

Belfast region

19th-century neo-Gothic cathedral that stands here today. ⓐ English Street ⓣ 028 4461 4922 ⓦ www.downcathedral.org ◷ 09.30–16.30 Mon–Sat, 14.00–17.00 Sun

Across the car park from the St Patrick Centre (see box) you'll see **Downpatrick Railway**, a historic steam railway that will take you to Inch Abbey. ⓐ Market Street ⓣ 028 4461 5779 ⓦ www.downrail.co.uk ◷ 13.40–17.00 specific days (see website or call for information) ⓘ Admission charge

Next to the cathedral, **Down County Museum** is located on the site of a former jail and military barracks where United Irishman Thomas Russell was hanged in 1803. Today, it houses a vast collection of archaeological and historic exhibits from the county. ⓐ The Mall, English Street ⓣ 028 4461 5218 ⓦ www.downcountymuseum.com ◷ 10.00–17.00 Mon–Fri, 13.00–17.00 Sat & Sun

Dundrum Castle

Originally built by John de Courcy in the 12th century, Dundrum is one of the finest Norman castles in Northern Ireland, with panoramic views of Dundrum Bay, the Mourne Mountains and the surrounding countryside. Climb the round keep for wonderful views. ⓐ Dundrum Village ⓣ 028 9181 1491 ⓦ www.ehsni.gov.uk ◷ 09.00–18.00 Tues–Sat, 13.00–18.00 Sun (Apr–Sept); 10.00–18.00 Sat (Oct–Mar) ⓝ Bus: Dundrum

Groomsport

A charming seaside village 3.2 km (2 miles) east of Bangor, with a harbour, sandy beach and plenty of pubs and restaurants. Once a fishing village, today it is a popular stop-off for day-

trippers and sailing enthusiasts. Look out for the whitewashed Cockle Row Cottages, home to fishermen at the beginning of the 20th century. ⓐ Groomsport ⓝ Bus: 3 (from Bangor)

Hillsborough

Several times voted the most beautiful village in Northern Ireland, Hillsborough doesn't disappoint, with pretty terraced cottages with hanging baskets, boutiques, cafés and pubs selling good grub. Behind the main square you'll find **Hillsborough Castle** (ⓐ The Square ⓣ 028 9268 1308), official residence of the Secretary of State for Northern Ireland.

IRELAND'S PATRON SAINT

Kidnapped from his home in Britain as a teenager, St Patrick spent six years as a slave in County Antrim, before escaping and becoming a missionary, returning to Ireland to convert the Irish to Christianity. According to legend, he taught the Irish people the concept of the Trinity using the three-leaved shamrock. At the bottom of Down Hill, where the cathedral stands, is the modern **St Patrick Centre**, where you can learn about the saint's history, browse the souvenirs in the shop and enjoy a cup of tea in the café. ⓐ 53A Lower Market Street ⓣ 028 4461 9000 ⓦ www.saintpatrickcentre.com ⓛ 10.00–17.00 Mon–Sat (Oct–Mar); 09.30–17.30 Mon–Sat, 13.00–17.30 Sun (Apr, May & Sept); 09.30–18.00 Mon–Sat, 10.00–18.00 Sun (June–Aug) ⓘ Admission charge

Unfortunately it's only open a few days a year. Head through the square and downhill and follow signs to Hillsborough Forest Park on the left-hand side. ⓐ Tourist Information, The Square, Hillsborough ⓣ 028 9268 9717 Bus: Hillsborough

Mourne Mountains

You don't have to be a hard-core hiker to appreciate the Mournes: this is, quite simply, one of the most stunning spots in Northern Ireland. For a lovely jaunt, drive to **Tollymore Forest Park** with its gentle woodland strolls, or bravely tackle **Slieve Donard**, Northern Ireland's highest peak. There are plenty of other outdoor activities here from canoeing to orienteering (see page 34). ⓐ Newcastle ⓦ www.mournemountains.com Bus: Newcastle

Cocklerow Cottage at Groomsport

Newcastle

A popular seaside resort at the foot of the mountains, Newcastle has a sweeping bay looking out to the Irish Sea. It's a good base for exploring the Mourne Mountains, and is home to the Royal County Down golf course. Bus: Newcastle

Strangford Lough

Strangford Lough is separated from the Irish Sea by the Ards Peninsula, a strip of land that extends south from Bangor to Portaferry. You can spend more than a day walking along nature trails and visiting all the attractions around the water. **Scrabo Hill Country Park**, northwest of the lough, is dominated by Scrabo Hill and the tower upon it, and there's a picnic site with great views over the lough (off the A22/A21 Tower 028 9181 1491 10.30–18.00 Sat–Thur, closed Fri).

At the southern tip of the lough, make a detour to see **Inch Abbey**, the ruins of a Cistercian abbey founded by John de Courcy in the 12th century. You can take the steam train from nearby Downpatrick (see page 105) through scenic countryside (off the Downpatrick–Belfast road open access all year). Heading east along the A25, you'll come to **Castle Ward**, an 18th-century country mansion set in a vast estate with formal gardens, woodland walks, a small petting farm, mill and superb views over the lough (Strangford 028 4488 1204 Guided tours of the house: 13.00–18.00 public holidays, school holidays & weekends (Mar–Sept); grounds: 10.00–20.00 (May–Sept); 10.00–16.00 (Oct–Apr) Bus: 16E from Downpatrick to Strangford).

From Strangford, there's a ferry to and from Portaferry. Here, the most popular attraction is **Exploris**, an aquarium with species

native to the shores of Northern Ireland, including bass, edible sea urchin, octopus and peacock worm. ⓐ The Rope Walk, Castle Street, Portaferry ⓣ 028 4272 8062 ⓦ www.exploris.org.uk
Ⓛ 10.00–18.00 Mon–Fri, 11.00–18.00 Sat, 12.00–18.00 Sun (Apr–Aug); 10.00–17.00 Mon–Fri, 11.00–17.00 Sat, 13.00–17.00 Sun (Sept–Mar) ⓘ Admission charge

CULTURE

Ulster Folk & Transport Museum

One of the most popular attractions in Northern Ireland, this museum is set in over 68 ha (170 acres) of countryside. The Folk Museum comprises buildings from all over the province that have been transported here, rebuilt and restored to give an authentic view of life in early 20th-century Ulster. In each cottage, mill and shop you'll meet 'residents' in period costume spinning at the wheel, cooking soda wheaten over the fire or serving behind the counter.

The Transport Museum has an impressive array of artefacts ranging from horse-drawn carts to Irish-built motor cars and locomotives. There is also a comprehensive display on the history of ship and aircraft building. You'll need a full day to get round the whole lot so bring a picnic, or enjoy a snack in the tearooms. ⓐ 153 Bangor Road, Cultra, Holywood
ⓣ 028 9042 8428 ⓦ www.uftm.org.uk ⓔ uftm.info@magni.org.uk
Ⓛ 10.00–17.00 Tues–Sun (Mar–Sept); 10.00–16.00 Tues–Fri, 11.00–16.00 Sat & Sun (Oct–Feb); closed Mon
Bus: Museum entrance; Train: Cultra Halt
ⓘ Admission charge

TAKING A BREAK

RESTAURANTS

Boyles ££ A combination of the chef's innovative use of Irish ingredients, the excellent service and traditional rustic décor have made this restaurant a hit. Sip locally made mead by the open fire then dine in the restaurant on Strangford langoustines, pot-roasted County Down rabbit and Portavogie smoked haddock

Bangor Marina

with spinach, mash and quail's egg. ⓐ 8 Castle Street, Dromore ⓣ 028 9269 9141 ⓦ www.boylesofdromore.com ⓒ 17.00–23.00 Tues & Thur, 12.00–01.00 Fri & Sat, 12.00–22.30 Sun

Mourne Seafood Bar ££ Some of the freshest seafood and fish dishes on the coast here. It even has its own mussel and oyster beds in Carlingford Lough and sells fresh fish to take home. ⓐ 77 Main Street, Dundrum ⓣ 028 4375 1377 ⓦ www.mourneseafood.com ⓒ 12.00–21.00 Mon–Fri, closed Sat & Sun; closed Mon & Tues off-season

The Old Inn ££ Located in Ireland's oldest coaching inn, the Gallery Restaurant serves a combination of classical and modern cuisine. Also offers a set-price menu for two in The Churn Bistro. ⓐ The Old Inn, Main Street, Crawfordsburn ⓣ 028 9185 3255 ⓦ www.theoldinn.com ⓒ 19.00–21.30 Mon–Sat, 12.30–14.30 Sun

Mitre Restaurant £££ Considered to be one of the best restaurants in Northern Ireland, with a fine-dining set menu. ⓐ Culloden Hotel, Bangor Road, Holywood ⓣ 028 9042 1066 ⓦ www.hastingshotels.com ⓒ 19.00–21.30 Mon–Sat, 12.30–14.30 & 19.00–21.00 Sun

ACCOMMODATION

HOTELS & GUESTHOUSES

Broadcove Cottage £ This white, traditional Irish-style cottage B&B is located at the foot of the Mourne Mountains just outside Newcastle and also boasts panoramic views over the sea. Comfortable and contemporary rooms make for a welcome retreat after a day's walking. ⓐ 93 Ballagh Road, Newcastle ⓣ 028 4372 7119 ⓦ www.broadcovecottage.co.uk

The Royal Hotel ££ Family-run hotel on Bangor seafront with café, bar and restaurant. ⓐ 26–28 Quay Street, Bangor ⓣ 028 9127 1866 ⓦ www.royalhotelbangor.com

The Old Inn £££ Located in Ireland's oldest coaching inn, famous guests are said to include the highwayman Dick Turpin and former US president, George Bush (senior). Stay in cosy rooms with four-poster beds. ⓐ Main Street, Crawfordsburn ⓣ 028 9185 3255 ⓦ www.theoldinn.com

Slieve Donard £££ Impressive Victorian hotel with views of the Mourne Mountains and the Irish Sea plus a luxury spa, a restaurant and a bar with live entertainment. ⓐ Downs Road, Newcastle ⓣ 028 4372 1066 ⓦ www.hastingshotels.com

CAMPING & HOSTELS

Mourneview Caravan Park £ One of many caravan parks positioned along the Dundrum Road, this one permits touring caravans and has its own hire facilities. ⓐ A2 from Newcastle to Dundrum ⓣ 028 4372 3327 ⓦ www.mourneview.net

Newcastle Hostel £ Located right on the seafront near pubs and restaurants. ⓐ 30 Downs Road, Newcastle ⓣ 028 4372 2133 ⓦ www.hini.org.uk (for booking)

Antrim Coast

The Antrim Coast is one of the most beautiful parts of Northern Ireland. It is a stunning coastline of lush forest glens, sweeping bays and turquoise seas during the summer, which in the winter becomes wild and romantic. Steeped in myth and legend with a history of settlement dating way back to the Neolithic era, there are many natural and man-made sights, including Giant's Causeway, Bushmills Distillery, Dunluce Castle, Carrick-a-Rede Rope Bridge and Rathlin Island. Even without so much to see and do, the drive itself takes in so much varied and spectacular scenery that it is not to be missed. Dotted with picture-postcard villages such as Cushendun and Ballintoy and the seaside towns of Ballycastle and Portrush, this really is a part of Northern Ireland that you'll never forget.

GETTING THERE

Hiring a car gives you the freedom to explore the Antrim Coast at your leisure. Drive north out of Belfast along the M2, then take the M5 towards Carrickfergus (about 20 minutes from the city centre). From there, take the A2 coast road. Ballintoy, Carrick-a-Rede, Giant's Causeway and Bushmills are all within 2 hours' drive, with Portrush a further 15 minutes away. Ulsterbus run the Antrim Coaster from Laganside Buscentre to Portrush and Coleraine via the coast road. There are trains from Belfast Central to Coleraine, where you can pick up another train or bus to your destination. **Caledonian MacBrayne** (ⓣ 028 2076 9299 ⓦ www.calmac.co.uk) operate around six ferries a day from Ballycastle to Rathlin Island during the summer months.

SIGHTS & ATTRACTIONS

Antrim Coast Road

The drive along the coastal road is breathtaking, with its craggy cliffs, pretty bays, glens and picturesque villages. You can drive along the coast on the A2 from Larne to Ballycastle, continuing along the coastal road after Cushendall or going cross-country to explore the Glens. Cushendall and Cushendun are among the prettiest villages. ⓐ A2 Antrim Coast Road Bus: Antrim Coaster (252), drive or tour

Bushmills Distillery

The oldest licensed whiskey distillery in the world, with a history dating back to 1608. You can take a tour around the distillery but it can get very busy; tickets are sold on a first-come, first-served basis. ⓐ Main Street, Bushmills ⓣ 028 2073 1521 ⓦ www.bushmills.com 09.15–16.00 Mon–Sat, 12.00–16.00 Sun (Mar–Oct) Bus: Bushmills Admission charge

Carrick-a-Rede Rope Bridge

Fight your fear of heights and take the challenge of walking across this rope bridge. Actually, it is much better than the original, which only had a single handrail. It was constructed by fishermen who wanted to cross to the rocky island to fish for salmon, but it was eventually taken over by the National Trust, which added the much safer bridge seen here today. Some people make it over to the other side only to panic and not be able to return – until the wardens tell them they will be winched up into a helicopter and then presented with the bill! ⓐ Whitepark Road, Ballintoy ⓣ 028 2076 9839 ⓦ www.nationaltrust.org.uk ◷ 10.00–18.00 (last tickets at 17.15) Feb–May, Sept & Oct; 10.00–19.00 (last tickets at 18.15) June–Aug; 10.30–15.30 (last tickets at 14.45) Nov–Dec (all opening hours are weather permitting) ❗ Admission charge

Carrickfergus Castle

A dominant feature of the coastal town of Carrickfergus and the site of many a battle, the castle has a colourful history dating back 800 years. The English retreated here during Edward the Bruce's invasion, and during the 14th century it fell to the Scots after a long siege. Over the years it has been used variously as a prison, a magazine and an air-raid shelter. ⓐ Marine Highway ⓣ 028 9335 1273 ⓦ www.ehsni.gov.uk

The breathtakingly beautiful coast at Giant's Causeway

10.00–16.00 Mon–Sat, 14.00–16.00 Sun (Oct–Mar); 10.00–18.00 Mon–Sat, 14.00–18.00 Sun (Apr–Sept) Train: Carrickfergus Admission charge

Dunluce Castle

The ruins of this medieval castle perch on the edge of the North Antrim cliffs between Bushmills and Portrush. During a storm in 1639 a whole section of the castle collapsed into the sea, killing the cooks and kitchen staff. The castle was abandoned and over time the entire building fell into disrepair. There's a visitor centre and shop, and tours around the castle. A2 Coast Road between Bushmills and Portrush 028 2073 1938 dunluce.castle@doeni.gov.uk 10.00–17.00 daily Drive or tour bus only Admission charge

Giant's Causeway

A must-see for anyone visiting the province, Giant's Causeway is one of Northern Ireland's top attractions and a UNESCO World Heritage Site. Until geologists came up with scientific theories on the origins of the strange hexagonal basalt columns, the area was steeped in myth and legend. The most famous story surrounds Fionn McCumhaill (McCool), a giant who fell in love with a Scottish belle and created a pathway to reach her. In reality, it's thought to have been the result of volcanic eruptions and the subsequent cooling of the lava by the sea. In total, there are around 40,000 columns of varying heights. Look out for the Giant's Boot, Organ, Chimney Stack and Camel's Back, among other features. You can walk the route from the visitor centre down to the Causeway and

Giant's Causeway: a must-see

ascend the cliffs, returning along the top. Alternatively, there is a bus that will take you to and from the main site. ⓐ 3.2 km (2 miles) east of Bushmills ⓣ 028 2073 1582 (visitor centre) ⓦ www.nationaltrust.org.uk ⓛ 10.00–17.00 daily ⓝ Bus: Antrim Coaster to Giant's Causeway

Giant's Causeway & Bushmills Railway

Running on the route of the original Causeway Tram, which closed in 1949, the line reopened in 2002. Riding the narrow-gauge steam train is a great way to travel between the two places. There are picnic areas, a café and a car park at the Giant's Causeway Station. A service is usually run during St Patrick's weekend, weekends from Easter until June, daily during July and August, and weekends during September and October. ⓐ Runkerry Road, Bushmills ⓣ 028 2073 2844 ⓘ Admission charge

Nine Glens of Antrim – Glenarm, Glencloy, Glenariff, Glenballyemon, Glenaan, Glencorp, Glendun, Glenshesk and Glentaisie

From the Antrim plateau to the Antrim Coast Road, the nine green Glens of Antrim are a rich mix of waterfalls, rivers, lush forests, peat bogs, flora and fauna. Glenariff Forest Park is one of the most beautiful areas, with walking trails leading past scenic mountain viewpoints. ⓐ Antrim Coast ⓝ Bus: Antrim Coaster; Car: A2

Portrush

A favourite holiday destination, Portrush is set in a wide, sweeping bay with sandy beaches. Local attractions include

THE GLENS OF ANTRIM: LAND OF MYTHS

Many legends have circulated the Glens of Antrim, from the Giant Fionn McCool to the Children of Lir (who were turned into swans by their evil stepmother, Aiofe). Make a detour from the Glenariff Forest Park to visit Slemish Mountain, where St Patrick is said to have tended Miliucc's sheep after he was captured and brought to Ireland. Watch out for the Watershee, a female fairy who is said to sing sweet songs to lure travellers into lakes and bogs before drowning them. And remember, never cut down a hawthorn tree or you'll upset the fairy folk and bad luck will surely follow. Whether you believe it or not, you'll find magical scenery and plenty of birdwatching, fishing and hiking.

Waterworld indoor water facility, Barry's Amusements (largest amusement park in Ireland) and the Countryside Centre (interactive marine exhibits). There's also surfing on the Blue Flag beaches, fishing on or off shore, tennis, bowling, golf at Royal Portrush, and coastal walking and cycling routes. ⓐ North Antrim Coast Bus: Dunluce Avenue

Rathlin Island

Located 10 km (6 miles) offshore from Ballycastle, Rathlin Island is 13 km (8 miles) long and less than 1.6 km (1 mile) wide. A birdwatchers' paradise, this is home to Northern Ireland's largest seabird colony – look out for razorbills, fulmars, guillemots and puffins from the RSPB viewpoint at the West Light. This lighthouse is one of three on the island: so wild is the coastline that over the years it has seen a total of about 40 shipwrecks. ⓐ 10 km (6 miles) off Ballycastle ⓣ 028 7032 7960 or 0774 556 6924 to arrange a tour with Paul Quinn Ferry: Ballycastle to Rathlin Island

Whitepark Bay & Ballintoy

This beautiful sweeping bay runs between the hamlet of Portbradden and Ballintoy and is one of the most popular walking routes in the area. The path winds along the basalt cliff top. Ballintoy itself is a picturesque village with its iconic white church and a limestone harbour sheltered by the cliffs behind. ⓐ North Antrim Coast Bus: Ballintoy

FESTIVALS

Some of the best festivals during the year include: Waterways Ireland Riverfest with two days of extreme water action on skis and jetskis (June); Larne Alive Festival, a month-long event with music, train rides, steam engines and circus acts (June); Feis na Gleann, a traditional Irish music festival throughout the glens (June); Ballycastle Fleadh, a weekend of traditional song and dance (June); Medieval Lughnasa Fayre in Carrickfergus with costumed performers (July); Heart of the Glens Festival in Cushendall with local singing and dance (August); and the Ould Lammas Fair in Ballycastle, one of the oldest in Ireland with livestock sales and stalls selling dulse (dried edible seaweed), and yellowman (a very sugary confectionery not unlike rock).

TAKING A BREAK

Many of the accommodation options below have restaurants, but there are also cafés and bars in every village along the Antrim Coast Road serving both lunch and dinner. Cushendall and Cushendun are among the prettiest villages, but there's more choice in places like Carrickfergus, Larne, Ballycastle and Portrush. Some of the main attractions, such as Giant's Causeway and Carrick-a-Rede Rope Bridge, have cafés where you can stop for refreshments.

AFTER DARK

RESTAURANTS & BARS

55° North £ Split-level family restaurant overlooking the sea that serves a wide range of contemporary dishes, from risotto of pan-seared scallops to braised lamb. In the summer, sit outside and enjoy the magnificent views. ⓐ 1 Causeway Street, Portrush ⓣ 028 7082 2811 ⓦ www.55-north.com ⓛ 12.00–15.00, 17.30–21.00 Tues–Fri, 10.00–21.00 Sat, 12.30–19.30 Sun, bar downstairs stays open until late Fri & Sat, closed Mon

The Distillers Arms £ Comfy pub in Bushmills where you can stop for a pint in front of the fire with lunch or dinner menus, including seafood chowder, fish and chips and home-cured Irish salmon. ⓐ Main Street ⓣ 028 2073 1044 ⓦ www.distillersarms.com ⓛ 12.00–late, food served 12.30–15.00 & 17.00–21.00 (summer); 17.00–late Mon–Fri, 11.00–late Sat & Sun, food served 17.30–21.00 Wed–Sat, 12.30–15.00 Sat & Sun (winter)

The Manor House £ A former Georgian gentleman's house, today it is a guesthouse and restaurant serving fresh fish. Dinner should be pre-ordered. ⓐ Rathlin Island ⓣ 028 2076 3964 ⓦ www.rathlinmanorhouse.co.uk ⓛ Dinner served at 19.00

The Nook at the Giant's Causeway £–££ Housed in a former 1850s schoolhouse, this restaurant offers a taste of Ulster and is renowned for its scones. ⓐ 48 Causeway Road ⓣ 028 2073 2993 ⓛ Restaurant: 12.00–21.00, bar: 11.30–23.00 Mon–Sat, 11.30–22.00 Sun

Central Wine Bar ££ Downstairs there's a restored traditional bar dating back to 1861 with regular traditional music and live bands. Upstairs has been transformed into a funky restaurant and wine bar serving modern Irish cuisine. ⓐ 12 Ann Street, Ballycastle ⓣ 028 2076 3877 ⓦ www.centralwinebar.com ⓛ Restaurant: 12.00–21.00, downstairs bar: 11.30–23.30

ACCOMMODATION

HOTELS AND GUESTHOUSES

The Burn £ Comfortable B&B in picturesque Cushendall. ⓐ 63 Ballyemon Road, Cushendall ⓣ 028 2177 1733 ⓦ www.theburn-guesthouse.com ⓔ theburn63@hotmail.com

The Causeway Hotel ££ B&B-style accommodation located right on the doorstep of Giant's Causeway, with superb views. ⓐ 40 Causeway Road, Bushmills ⓣ 028 2073 1210 ⓕ 028 2073 2552 ⓦ www.giants-causeway-hotel.com

Smugglers Inn ££ B&B near Giant's Causeway with a restaurant, bar and even its own distillery. ⓐ 306 Whitepark Road ⓣ 028 2073 1577 ⓦ www.smugglers-inn.co.uk ⓔ jenny@smugglers-inn.co.uk

Ballygally Castle £££ Located on the Antrim Coast Road at the foot of the Glens of Antrim, this hotel looks out to the Irish Sea. Part of the hotel dates back to the 17th century and is said to be haunted by a friendly ghost. ⓐ Coast Road, Ballygally ⓣ 028 2858 1066 ⓦ www.hastingshotels.com

The Marine Hotel £££ Comfortable hotel overlooking Ballycastle's new harbour and marina, with restaurant, bar and entertainment. ⓐ 1–3 North Street, Ballycastle ⓣ 028 2076 2222 ⓦ www.marinehotel.net

CAMPING AND HOSTELS

Cushendall Caravan Park £ Camping on the Antrim Coast Road. ⓐ 62 Coast Road, Cushendall ⓣ 028 2177 1699

Cushendun Caravan Park £ Small, family-run caravan park further along the coast. ⓐ 14 Glendun Road, Cushendun ⓣ 028 2176 1254

Mill Rest Youth Hostel £ Cheap and basic accommodation for those on a budget. ⓐ 49 Main Street, Bushmills ⓣ 028 2073 1222 ⓦ www.hini.org.uk ⓔ millrest@hini.org.uk

---

The Cathedral Quarter is Belfast's historic heart

PRACTICAL information

Directory

GETTING THERE

By air

Both of Belfast's nearby airports are served by a number of budget airlines. Frequent Airport Express services mean both are well connected to the city centre. Aer Lingus operates daily flights between Belfast International and London Heathrow. BMI Baby operates several flights a day between Belfast International Airport and Birmingham, Cardiff, Manchester and Nottingham East Midlands. EasyJet operates several flights a day between Belfast International and Bristol, Edinburgh, Glasgow, Liverpool, London (Gatwick, Luton and Stansted) and Newcastle, and daily flights between George Best Belfast City Airport and London Luton. Jet2.com operates daily flights between Belfast International, Blackpool and Leeds Bradford, as well as twice-weekly flights to Newquay. Manx2.com operates daily (except Sat) flights from George Best Belfast City Airport to Blackpool and Cork and Galway, and several daily flights to the Isle of Man. It also operates a weekly service between Belfast International and Blackpool, and daily (except Sat) flights to the Isle of Man. British Airways operates several flights a day between George Best Belfast City Airport and Manchester. Flybe operates several flights a day between Belfast City and Aberdeen, Birmingham, Cardiff, Doncaster Sheffield, Dundee, Edinburgh, Exeter, Glasgow, Inverness, Jersey, Leeds Bradford, London Gatwick, Manchester, Newcastle, Newquay and Southampton, and a daily flight to and from Bristol.

Aer Lingus ⓣ 0871 718 5000 ⓦ www.aerlingus.com

bmibaby 0905 828 2828 www.bmibaby.com
British Airways 0844 493 0787 www.ba.com
easyJet 0905 821 0905 www.easyjet.com
flybe 0871 700 2000 www.flybe.com
Jet2.com 0871 226 1737 www.jet2.com
Manx2.com 0871 200 0440 www.manx2.com

Many people are aware that air travel emits CO_2, which contributes to climate change. You may be interested in the possibility of lessening the environmental impact of your flight through the charity **Climate Care** (www.jpmorganclimatecare.com), which offsets your CO_2 by funding environmental projects around the world.

By rail

Services to Belfast run from Bangor, Derry City and Portrush, Larne and Portadown. There's also the cross-border Enterprise service with Iarnród Éireann eight times a day between Belfast and Dublin with main Northern Ireland stops at Derry, Coleraine, Belfast Central, Lisburn, Portadown and Newry.

By road

Scottish Citylink runs services between Belfast's Europa Buscentre and various Scottish cities (www.citylink.co.uk). **National Express** runs services between the Europa Buscentre and several English and Welsh cities (www.nationalexpress.com).

Belfast is 113 km (70 miles) from Derry by A roads and the M2 motorway, 160 km (100 miles) from Dublin and 422 km (262 miles) from Cork on toll-paying motorways, A roads and the M1 motorway into Belfast city centre.

By water

There are several ferry routes from the rest of the UK that come into Belfast ferry port close to the city centre and Larne (37 km (23 miles), north of Belfast). **Stena Line** operates regular Belfast–Stranraer, Belfast–Troon and Larne (north of Belfast)–Fleetwood services (Ⓦ www.stenaline.co.uk). **Steam Packet** operates a Belfast–Douglas (Isle of Man) service (Ⓦ www.steam-packet.com). **P&O Irish Sea Ferries** operates Larne–Troon and Larne–Cairnryan services (Ⓦ www.poirishsea.com). **Norfolkline Irish Sea** operates a Belfast–Liverpool service (Ⓦ www.norfolkline-ferries.co.uk).

ENTRY FORMALITIES

UK citizens need some form of photographic ID (usually a valid passport or driving licence). Citizens of EU countries, USA, Canada, Australia, New Zealand and South Africa do not require a visa if coming to Northern Ireland as a visitor.

Visitors to the UK and Northern Ireland are entitled to bring the following duty-paid goods into the country for their own personal use: up to 3,200 cigarettes, 400 cigarillos, 200 cigars, 3 kg of smoking tobacco, 10 litres of spirits, 90 litres of wine (60 litres of sparkling wine), 20 litres of fortified wine and 110 litres of beer. However, if you are questioned by Customs officials and cannot satisfy them that it is not for commercial use, it could be seized and not returned. Exceptions apply to the following EU countries: from Estonia, 200 cigarettes or 250 g of smoking tobacco (no restrictions on other tobacco products if for your own use); from Bulgaria, Hungary, Latvia, Lithuania, Poland, Slovakia and Slovenia, 200 cigarettes (no restrictions on other tobacco products if for your own use).

If you are travelling from a non-EU country you have a duty-free allowance of 200 cigarettes or 100 cigarillos or 50 cigars or 250 g of tobacco; 2 litres of still table wine; 1 litre of spirits or strong liqueurs over 22 per cent volume or 2 litres of fortified wine, sparkling wine or other liqueurs; 60 cc/ml of perfume; 250 cc/ml of eau de toilette and £145 worth of all other goods, including gifts and souvenirs.

MONEY

As with the rest of the UK, in Northern Ireland the currency is UK pounds sterling. Northern Ireland has four clearing banks – Bank of Ireland, First Trust, Northern Bank and Ulster Bank, which print their own banknotes. These are valid sterling notes in the same denominations as the rest of the UK (£5, £10, £20 and £50) but it's advisable to change them to English notes if you're moving on to England as many places don't like to accept them, despite their legality. Most banks have ATMs and are located throughout the city centre, main commercial areas of the city and all towns throughout the province. Larger banks in Belfast have bureaux de change, but you can also try travel agencies, the Belfast Welcome Centre, some tourist information centres, large hotels and some tourist attractions.

Credit cards are generally accepted in most shops, restaurants, bars and attractions, but if there's any doubt, it is best to check first to avoid any embarrassment.

HEALTH, SAFETY & CRIME

There should be absolutely no problem with the drinking water in Belfast – the main supply comes from the Mourne Mountains. Likewise, there should be no problem with the city's food.

The public health-care system in Northern Ireland is part of the UK National Health Service (NHS) but here it integrates both health and social care into one system, so citizens of the UK are covered for health care. As part of a reciprocal agreement, citizens of the EU are entitled to reduced-cost and sometimes free medical treatment if they have a European Health Insurance Card (EHIC). You can apply for this in your country of citizenship. Make sure you have ID with you as well as your EHIC.

As an EHIC may not cover all your medical needs, it is always advisable to have your own private travel insurance to pay for repatriation, should you need it. Insurance also usually covers you if you are a victim of crime, but check your policy carefully before you travel.

Northern Ireland has one of the lowest crime rates in Europe. Even during the Troubles tourists were rarely targeted or directly affected. Just use your common sense as you would when travelling anywhere – don't take too much cash out with you, don't flash expensive jewellery around or walk along the street with a big open map. It can also get quite rowdy at the weekends along the Golden Mile and Botanic but most people are just happy after a few drinks. However, if you're lost or feel uncomfortable it's better to ask someone for directions during the day – most people are happy to help – or take a taxi home if it's late; try **Fon A Cab** (028 9023 3333). If you do have an emergency, call the police, ambulance or fire service on 999. For lost valuables, call the **PSNI (Police Service of Northern Ireland) Police Lost Property** (0845 600 8000 non-emergency police number). Alternatively, you can call into Musgrave Police Station on Ann Street (by Queen's Bridge) for this or other matters.

OPENING HOURS

Shops usually open from Monday to Saturday 09.30–17.30 with late-night shopping on Thursday (until 21.00). Larger stores and most high-street shops in Belfast city centre also open on Sunday from 13.00–18.00. Banks generally open from Monday to Friday 09.30–16.30 but some also open on Saturday mornings. Banks are always closed on Sundays and public holidays.

TOILETS

There are several public toilets in the city centre either as standalones in the street or in car parks, bus stations (Europa

The city centre is easy to navigate

and Laganside Buscentres), shopping centres and markets, including CastleCourt on Royal Avenue. You can also find clean toilets in department stores and museums, and McDonald's in Royal Avenue is also widely used, although it's not the cleanest of places. In an emergency you can also go into pubs and cafés, but they'll usually want you to buy something first.

CHILDREN

Children are welcomed and allowed in more establishments than in England, but in general they are not allowed in bars and pubs, unless they serve food as well (the bars, not the children).

Children should love going on sightseeing bus tours, boat trips and to the Odyssey Centre (see pages 92–3), where there's all-day entertainment, including the W5 interactive discovery centre and the Pavilion. A great fresh-air idea is Belfast Castle (see pages 75 & 78) and Cave Hill Country Park (see page 80). If there aren't any events on at the castle you can have a look around, then take the kids on a nature trail through the park up to the gloriously named Napoleon's Nose. Titanic Boat Tours allow children to discover something about the *Titanic* and enjoy the short boat trip at the same time (see page 94).

COMMUNICATIONS

Internet

Belfast is well wired. The Belfast Welcome Centre (see page 136) is a reliable and pleasant place to check those stress-inducing emails from the boss.

TELEPHONING THE UK

The Belfast and other Northern Ireland numbers in this book include the Northern Ireland number (028) followed by an area code and a six-digit number. Within Northern Ireland you don't need to dial 028 but you do need to dial the rest of the digits.

TELEPHONING ABROAD

To phone anywhere else you should dial the national code first (353 Republic of Ireland, 1 USA or Canada, 61 Australia, 64 New Zealand and 72 South Africa) plus the area code (minus the 0 if there is one) and the rest of the number. For international operator assistance, call 155.

Phone

Coin- and card-operated telephone booths can be found all over the city. Phone cards can be purchased at newsagents and supermarkets. All phones can be used to call abroad – it's cheaper before 08.00, after 18.00 and at weekends.

Post

Post offices are generally open from 09.00–17.30 Monday–Friday and 09.00–12.00 on Saturdays. The main post office in Belfast city centre is at Castle Junction. You can post your letters at post offices or in the red post boxes around the city and the rest of Northern Ireland. Stamps can be bought at post offices, newsagents, supermarkets and some tourist offices and petrol stations.

ELECTRICITY

As with the rest of the UK and Republic of Ireland, the current is 240V (50Hz) and three-pin plugs are used. Visitors from outside the UK or Ireland will need an adaptor.

TRAVELLERS WITH DISABILITIES

To stay in line with EU regulations, facilities are being improved in Northern Ireland as with the rest of the UK. Work on some venues has already taken place (Grand Opera House and large hotels and restaurants), providing wheelchair access via ramps or lifts. Sources of advice for travellers with disabilities include:

Shopmobility Belfast ⓐ Westgate House, 2 Queen Street ⓣ 028 9080 8090 ⓦ www.shopmobilitybelfast.co.uk

Disability Action ⓐ 189 Airport Road West ⓣ 028 9029 7880 ⓦ www.disabilityaction.org

TOURIST INFORMATION

Belfast has a very helpful tourist office in the city centre as well as two at Belfast International and George Best Belfast City Airport.

Belfast Welcome Centre ⓐ 47 Donegall Place ⓣ 028 9024 6609 ⓔ info@belfastvisitor.com ⓛ 09.00–17.30 Mon–Sat (Oct–May); 09.00–19.00 Mon–Sat, 12.00–17.00 Sun (June–Sept)

Useful websites include the official tourism website for Belfast, ⓦ www.gotobelfast.com, and the Discover Northern Ireland site, ⓦ www.discovernorthernireland.com

BACKGROUND READING

Belfast: A History by William A Maguire. A comprehensive history of Belfast and its people, the origins of religious divisions, the rise of shipbuilding and the building of RMS *Titanic*.

Belfast Diary: War as a Way of Life by John Conroy. An intimate account of growing up in West Belfast.

Great Hatred, Little Room: Making Peace in Northern Ireland by Jonathan Powell. An insider's account of the triumph of sacrifice, diplomacy and compromise that achieved what many had given up as impossible: the provision of peace to this beautiful city.

Made in Belfast by Vivienne Pollock and Trevor Parkhill. A good overview of life, work and industry, from the linen mills and shipbuilding to entertainments, with plenty of old photographs.

Troubled Images: Posters and Images of the Northern Ireland Conflict from the Linen Hall Library, Belfast by Yvonne Murphy, Allan Leonard, Gordon Gillespie and Kris Brown. This excellent collection contains some truly breathtaking illustrations of the city's long history of internecine struggle.

Watching the Door by Kevin Myers. A brilliantly executed, laugh-out-loud account of a young man's romp through the city during the Troubles.

The Wee Wild One: Stories of Belfast and Beyond by Ruth C Schwertfiger. A fresh view on the city through literature and strange tales.

Emergencies

EMERGENCY NUMBERS

For emergencies requiring police, fire or ambulance services, call ⓣ 999

MEDICAL SERVICES

Only call 999 in an absolute emergency. If you can, ask a pharmacist for help or visit a doctor's surgery. In case of emergency you should ask to be taken to the nearest hospital. The Royal has a specialist hospital just for children, as well as maternity and dentistry hospitals. Citizens of the UK are entitled to full medical treatment, and holders of EHICs (see page 132) are entitled to basic medical treatment. Still, travel insurance with a good level of medical cover is advisable for repatriation and essential for non-EU visitors.

Emergency medical services are very good in Northern Ireland and often the waiting time in A&E (Accident and Emergency) is less than in other UK hospitals. You should try to provide as much information as possible about the patient, including personal details and the symptoms. If you are physically able, go to A&E at the nearest hospital, or ask the hotel or pharmacist for the number of a local doctor, clinic or dentist.

Belfast City Hospital ⓐ 51 Lisburn Road ⓣ 028 9032 9241
Mater Hospital Trust ⓐ 45–51 Crumlin Road ⓣ 028 9074 1211
Royal Victoria Hospital ⓐ 274 Grosvenor Road ⓣ 028 9024 0503
Shaftesbury Square Hospital ⓐ 116–120 Great Victoria Street ⓣ 028 9032 9808

POLICE

If you are unlucky enough to be the victim of crime, you should call the **PSNI** (Police Service of Northern Ireland ⓣ 0845 600 8000). Only call 999 in absolute emergencies, otherwise contact the police station in person or by phone. If you lose some property or have something stolen, then you should report this to the lost property office at Musgrave Police Station. You'll be given an official report to help make any necessary insurance claims. It is advisable to take some photographic ID with you when you make the report.

Musgrave Police Station ⓐ Ann Street

EMBASSIES & CONSULATES

Australian High Commission ⓐ Australia House, Strand, London WC28 4LA ⓣ 020 7379 4334

Canadian Consulate ⓐ Unit 3, Ormeau Business Park ⓣ/ⓕ 028 9127 2060

New Zealand Honorary Consul ⓐ 118A Lisburn Road, Crumlin ⓣ 028 9264 8098

South African High Commission ⓐ South Africa House, Trafalgar Square, London ⓣ 020 7451 7299

US Consulate ⓐ Danesfort House, 223 Stranmillis Road ⓣ 028 9038 6100 ⓕ 028 9068 1301

ACKNOWLEDGEMENTS

The publishers would like to thank the following individuals and organisations for supplying their copyright photographs for this book: Apartment, pages 26–7; Belfast Tourist Office, pages 8 & 32; BigStockPhoto.com, pages 23 & 62 (Brendan Montgomery); Dreamstime.com, page 95 (Peter Clark); iStockphoto.com, page 5 (Robert Mayne); Louise McGrath, pages 38, 103, 118, 120 & 127; Waterfront Hall, page 19, Christopher Holt, all others.

Project Editor: Kate Taylor
Proofreaders: Caroline Hunt & Jan McCann
Layout: Donna Pedley

Send your thoughts to
books@thomascook.com

- **Found a great bar, club, shop or must-see sight that we don't feature?**
- **Like to tip us off about any information that needs a little updating?**
- **Want to tell us what you love about this handy little guidebook and more importantly how we can make it even handier?**

Then here's your chance to tell all! Send us ideas, discoveries and recommendations today and then look out for your valuable input in the next edition of this title.

Email the above address (stating the title) or write to:
pocket guides Series Editor, Thomas Cook Publishing, PO Box 227, Coningsby Road, Peterborough PE3 8SB, UK.

WHAT'S IN YOUR GUIDEBOOK?

Independent authors Impartial up-to-date information from our travel experts who meticulously source local knowledge.

Experience Thomas Cook's 165 years in the travel industry and guidebook publishing enriches every word with expertise you can trust.

Travel know-how Thomas Cook has thousands of staff working around the globe, all living and breathing travel.

Editors Travel-publishing professionals, pulling everything together to craft a perfect blend of words, pictures, maps and design.

You, the traveller We deliver a practical, no-nonsense approach to information, geared to how you really use it.

ABOUT THE AUTHOR

Based in County Down, Northern Ireland, Louise McGrath (aka Pole-Baker) is a freelance writer/editor and the author of Thomas Cook's *pocket guides Belfast* and *Lisbon*. Louise writes regularly for *www.whatsonwhen.com*, working on web content for major airlines and hotel chains. She has lived in Colombia, Spain and Florida, and in her spare time likes to walk in the Mourne Mountains, practise yoga and listen to live music.

Thomas Cook **pocket** guides

PARIS